Author

This guide was written by Kerry Lewis, author of *Mr Bruff's Guide to Grammar*. She has been a member of the mrbruff.com team since May 2014. You can follow Kerry on Twitter @Mrs_SPaG.

FREE EBOOK

The eBook edition of this guide is presented in colour. Whilst this print guide is completely accessible without colour, we would be happy to send you a free eBook if you email proof of purchase to info@mrbruff.com.

Dedications

Kerry Lewis would like to thank Andrew Simmons for volunteering his free time to read and comment on the final draft of this book. As usual, his erudite thoughts and comments have been extremely helpful and most gratefully received. Kerry would also like to thank Rowena Cole for her support: without Rowena, both this book and Mr Bruff's Guide to Grammar would not have been possible.

Mr Bruff would like to thank Sunny Ratilal and Sam Perkins, who worked on the front cover design.

Amazon Reviews of First Edition

This book is amazing! Not only does it talk about the (correct) terminology and language (an abundance more awaits in the book) that is vital for success at A' level, but it also gives an array of detail and examples to help the reader[...] It truly is a 'sound investment for your future'.

Luke Lamb

The guide is detailed, easy to understand and concise and, as well as providing information about context, literary theory, literary movements and terminology required for A' level English literature, the guide provides detailed information about assessment objectives and exactly what you need to include in your essays to get the top grades, a feature which seems to be unique to this guide and is sure to be beneficial [...] I would thoroughly recommend the guide to anyone, and consider it a must have for A' Level English literature!

Margaret Herdman

Would recommend this book to anyone studying English literature. It's a great resource for understanding the subject and technique. I am currently studying English literature and this book is helping me settle in to the subject and most of all enjoy the subject.

Amber

I took a gamble ordering this as it's not part of the traditional learning guides recommended for my A' level English literature and language. I was amazed at how quickly it helped me to get a really good grade in my coursework. I'm a pure online student, so doing my own research is time-consuming on what to read and how to get prepared for exam questions. This book, however, deals with all the topics as if you have access to a teacher, not a text book, in a very quick and concise way. I've found it very useful and the format as ebook was an added benefit as I got it within 2 minutes...Thank you!!

Ruwanthi

Contents

Introduction

First of all, congratulations on choosing to study English literature at AS or A' Level! Both qualifications aim to produce confident, critical students who can express original ideas. This is excellent preparation for university.

Whether you choose the AS or A' Level route, this practical ebook is relevant to all of the exam boards because their A' levels in English literature have the same assessment objectives.

There's a big gap between GCSE and A' level, and we want to help you to bridge that gap. Be aware that there's a lot packed into the pages that follow. Don't let this put you off! Think of this guide as a reference book containing helpful advice and practical examples: dip into it if you're not sure what a particular assessment objective means or if you're not sure how to approach a task.

In this updated edition of the ebook, references to the legacy specification have been removed. If you are beginning an AS or A' level in English literature, you should be tailoring your work to the assessment objectives below, which came into effect in September 2015.

Assessment Objectives*

AO1	Articulate informed, personal and creative responses to literary texts, using associated concepts and terminology, and coherent, accurate written expression.
AO2	Analyse ways in which meanings are shaped in literary texts.
AO3	Demonstrate understanding of the significance and influence of the contexts in which literary texts are written and received.
AO4	Explore connections across literary texts.
AO5	Explore literary texts informed by different interpretations.

This table contains public sector information licensed under the Open Government Licence v3.0.

The chapters in this ebook focus on the above assessment objectives.

IMPORTANT NOTE ON ASSESSMENT OBJECTIVES

You might not be assessed on every AO in every unit that you study; your teacher should provide you with more details. You can also check your exam board's specification online.

NOTE ON PUNCTUATION

The exam boards lack consistency with abbreviating *Advanced levels*. You might come across the hyphenated *A-levels* or the letter *A* as in *A levels*.

The word *Advanced* abbreviates to *A'* and the apostrophe shows that the letters *dvanced* are missing. As an ardent supporter of the Apostrophe Protection Society, I'm using the apostrophe to show that *Advanced* is abbreviated.

FINAL IMPORTANT NOTE:

This ebook is not endorsed by or affiliated to any exam boards. The writer is simply an experienced teacher, using her expertise to help students.

Chapter 1

Building on GCSE English Literature

When you were preparing for your GCSE exams, you might have bought revision guides to help you with particular texts. You're probably familiar with the excellent range of ebooks, for example, that Mr Bruff and his team have written.

Unfortunately, you can't depend solely on these for A' level English literature. If you do this, you won't gain a high mark.

Your informed thoughts about the texts are far more important. This is the difference between GCSE and A' level English literature.

At A' level, you're expected to give an informed personal response. This means that you become more of an independent learner, so there's more emphasis on research. To support your classroom studies, you'll be reading around the texts and demonstrating how your new knowledge informs your views. You'll learn fascinating facts about the contexts in which the texts were written and understood. You'll also learn critical theory and how to apply it. Finally, you'll research the views of other people, consider what they say and decide whether or not you agree with them. All of your wider reading will help you to argue your point of view—in an informed and knowledgeable way.

It goes without saying that these excellent research skills are invaluable for university.

A' level literature also prepares you for higher education by developing your essay writing skills. This guide teaches you how to reference your wider reading, write footnotes and a bibliography. You'll be using these skills in the non-examined component of your course.

Before we focus on the assessment objectives, however, we need to explore the requirements of independent reading in more detail.

Chapter 2

Independent Reading

This might be stating the obvious but, as an A' level literature student, you're expected to like reading!

As part of your programme of wider reading, you might sample texts of a particular genre or literary movement. Alternatively, you might choose to read texts with a similar theme to the ones that you are studying in class. You might also investigate historical events, cultural references and political movements—the list is endless.

It's impossible to do all of this reading within the classroom, so how much of your free time should you dedicate to this?

Different schools have different policies. Some recommend a minimum of five hours of independent study a week; others recommend double this number. Bear in mind that the more you read, the more you increase your chances of success.

The process of reading around a text isn't as arduous as it might sound: many students relish it because it's interesting and rewarding. It also develops their confidence when discussing texts and producing informed personal responses.

If the thought of independent study leaves you cold, however, just remember that A' levels are your passport to university, a well-paid job and a good lifestyle.

In short, independence.

Think about where you want to be in 2 - 5 years' time. Every time you don't want to do that independent reading, look at your goals.

Then read.

A' levels are only two years of your life.

They're worth the effort.

Chapter 3

AO1: Writing Skills and Language Terminology

Assessment Objective 1 (AO1) requires you to:

> **Articulate informed, personal and creative responses to literary texts, using associated concepts and terminology, and coherent, accurate written expression.**

But what does this mean? Let's examine one clause at a time.

Articulate Informed, Personal and Creative Responses to Literary Texts

This means that the examiner is assessing your critical understanding of the text(s) that you are studying.

In an academic context, 'critical' is a word that describes how you think. It doesn't mean being negative just for the sake of it. You have to consider your points carefully and express an evidence-based point of view that might agree or disagree with part or all of an exam question. Your response should be:

Informed: you know the text very well and have reflected upon the thoughts and ideas that it contains. This has involved analysing and evaluating different ideas and positions.

Personal: once you are informed, you are now in a position to think for yourself, ask questions about the text, evaluate ideas, and express your point of view.

Creative: you are showing the examiner that you are actively engaged with the text. You have thought carefully about the text and are expressing your own ideas, thereby providing evidence of independent thought.

Always remember to link your ideas to the question: don't write everything that you know about the text, regardless of relevance. Also consider a *yes, but* or *no, but* approach to answering questions, as this is a good way to demonstrate your informed, personal and creative ideas.

Using Associated Concepts and Terminology

The examiner is assessing your knowledge of concepts. **This means your knowledge of ideas and theories; for example, ideas associated with** *ballad,* *narrative method* **and** *comedy.* **If I were to demonstrate my knowledge of ballads, I might talk about their history, common themes, their structure and rhyme scheme. These are all** associated concepts.

Literary **terminology** is technical vocabulary that is used to analyse literary texts; for example, *simile, onomatopoeia* and *metaphor.* In this chapter, we'll review and hopefully extend your knowledge of terminology in more detail.

Why is knowledge of literary terminology so important? If you use it accurately and appropriately, you are demonstrating an academic style of writing.

You should be familiar with some of the following terminology from your GCSEs in English literature and English language, but other terminology and concepts might be new.

IMPORTANT! This guide aims to be a handy <u>reference</u> book so that you can dip into it when you need to check something. There's a lot of terminology in this chapter: don't panic! Your teacher should advise you on which is the most relevant for the particular text that you are studying.

BASIC GRAMMATICAL TERMINOLOGY

Adjective: describes a noun or pronoun. For example: *A <u>happy</u> student is smiling* OR *He is <u>happy</u>.*

Adverb: describes a verb. For example: *She walks <u>slowly</u> to school.*

Clause: part of a sentence. A **main clause** makes sense by itself because it has a subject and verb (for example, *I sang*). A compound sentence has two subjects and two verbs, creating two **independent clauses** (*I sang, so the window shattered*). A **subordinate clause** does not make sense by itself (*I sang, <u>thinking about my cat.</u>*) There are also **relative clauses**, which are like subordinate clauses except they are introduced by relative pronouns. For example: *I sang a song, <u>which made everyone cry</u>. I stared at the people, <u>who asked me to stop singing</u>.*

Conjunction: a word that joins sentences together. You might be familiar with the FANBOY conjunctions *for, and, nor, but, or, yet, so* which join independent clauses to make compound sentences.

Determiner: introduces a noun. For example: *a, the, this, that, these, those*.

Interjection: expresses sudden feelings and emotions. For example: *Wow!*

Noun: the name of a thing. **Abstract nouns** are things that you cannot touch, see, smell, hear or taste; for example, *beauty, love* and *anger*. **Collective nouns** describe a group of things; for example, *a gaggle of geese, an anthology of poems* and *a staff of teachers*. You can touch, see, smell, hear or taste **concrete nouns** such as c*hair, keyboard* and *water*. Finally, **proper nouns** are the names of specific people, places, organisations or things. They always begin with a capital letter: *Jim Smith, Swansea, Buckingham Palace and the Statue of Liberty.*

Object: receives the action of a verb. There is a **direct object** and an **indirect object**. For example: *She gives a <u>book</u>* (direct object) to *<u>him</u>* (indirect object).

Preposition: tells you where something is. For example: *The cat sat <u>on</u> the mat.*

Pronoun: takes the place of a noun. For example: *I, you, he, she, it, we and they.*

Participle: a verb that behaves like an adjective; for example, *a <u>smiling</u> boy*. The – ing part of a verb is a **present participle** and it shows an unfinished action. For example: *They are <u>whistling</u> merrily, <u>walking</u> to school and <u>looking</u> forward to their English lesson.* There are also **past participles**, which usually end in *-ed* if they are regular. These show that something has just been completed *(they have <u>finished</u> their lesson)* or has been done at some unspecified point in your life (*I've <u>visited</u> Spain a lot*). Finally, past participles are used in passive sentences, as in *the book was <u>finished</u>.*

Sentence: a group of words that begin with a capital letter and end with a full stop. At the barest minimum, a sentence has a subject and verb although this is not the case with minor sentences or fragments (for example: *Shocking.*) There are simple, compound and complex sentences as well as compound-complex sentences that contain at least two independent clauses and at least two subordinate clauses. For example:

<u>We downloaded some books</u> because they were cheaper than hard copies, and <u>we also wanted to travel light</u> when we went on holiday.

The independent clauses make sense by themselves and are underlined. The FANBOYS conjunction 'and' joins the two halves of the sentences. The remaining two phrases do not make sense by themselves and are therefore subordinate clauses.

Subject: The person, thing or place that the verb in a sentence is about. For example: *We went on holiday.*

Syntax: the way that words and phrases are arranged to create sentences. The syntax of an active sentence, for example, is *subject, verb, object* for example, (the dog eats the bone) while the syntax of a passive sentence is *object, verb* and sometimes *subject* (the bone is eaten by the dog).

Verb: a word that describes an action (for example, *run*), state (*be*) or occurrence *(happen).*

FIGURATIVE LANGUAGE

Figurative language takes you beyond the literal meaning of a word to provide you with new insights and understandings about meaning. You should be familiar with some of the examples below.

Allegory: a type of **extended metaphor** (see below), where you say one thing but mean another, over an extended length of time. An allegory is usually a fable or story, which has another meaning beyond the obvious surface meaning. C.S. Lewis's *The Lion, the Witch and the Wardrobe* is a religious allegory, in which Aslan is Jesus and Edmund is Judas.

Alliteration: the repetition of words that begin with the same sound. For example: *The swans are swimming to Sandra the psychology teacher.*

Allusion: an indirect reference to something or someone famous. It does not explicitly name the thing or person. For example, the expression *your nose is growing* is an allusion to the children's story *Pinocchio*, whose hero's nose grows whenever he tells a lie.

Assonance: the repetition of the same vowel sounds, but the consonants surrounding the vowels are different. For example: *Dented wedding bells.*

Consonance: the repetition of the same consonant sound in different words. (This is not to be confused with alliteration, which focuses on sounds at the beginnings of words.) This example is consonance: *His resolution to save her soul is lessening.*

Euphemism: a mild word or expression that replaces something quite harsh or blunt. For example: *My cat has <u>passed away</u>* (instead of 'died').

Hyperbole: deliberate exaggeration for emphasis. For example: *His incredibly loud sneeze blew me to the other end of the room.*

Idiom: an expression that has a different meaning to its literal meaning. For example: *He kicked the bucket.*

Imagery: figurative language that generates ideas, mental images, sensations and emotions. All the examples in this section apply.

Irony: where the speaker means the opposite to what he or she says. An example of **verbal irony** might be *he works really hard*, which means *he's lazy*. This might be interpreted as sarcasm. The main difference is that with sarcasm the speaker intends to hurt the other person's feelings. **Situational irony** is best understood by examining the context that people are in; for example, sailors stranded at sea will be surrounded by water, and yet might be dying of thirst, unable to drink the seawater. With **dramatic irony**, the audience knows something that the characters on the stage do not. For example, in *Romeo and Juliet*, Romeo believes that Juliet is dead, but the audience knows that she is in a drugged sleep.

Litotes: to deliberately understate a point in order to emphasise it. For example: *I'm not unhappy with my exam result.*

Metaphor: when you compare two things by saying that one thing is another. For example: *My brother's a pig.* He is not literally a pig with four legs and a curly tail, but the metaphor conjures up the idea of a lazy, gluttonous person.

An **extended metaphor** is when a metaphor is used and developed during a literary work, usually an entire poem. For example, *The Road Not Taken* by Robert Frost is an extended metaphor for the choices we take in life.

Metonymy: a replacement word that has close associations with the original. For example, *Downing Street* is a metonym for the Prime Minister; *suits* is a metonym for business people; and *Scotland Yard* is a metonym for London-based or British detectives.

Personification: where something non-human is described as if it is human. For example: *The inquisitive tree tapped its branches on my bedroom window.*

Onomatopoeia: where the sound of a word suggests its meaning. For example: *I can hear the ticking of a clock.*

Oxymoron: deliberately putting together two words that don't agree with each other. For example: *unfriendly smile, deafening silence* and *living dead.*

Paradox: a statement that seemingly contradicts itself. For example: 'I can resist anything but temptation.' *Oscar Wilde*

Pun: a deliberate play on words, usually to create humour. For example: *I wondered why the football was getting bigger. Then it hit me.*

Pathetic fallacy: where the setting reflects the mood of the character(s). For example: *While it was raining outside, the girl was sobbing uncontrollably.*

Rhetorical question: a question where no answer is expected.

Sibilance: most commonly, the repetition of the soft –s and –sh sounds in words. For example: 'And the silken sad uncertain rustling of each purple curtain' (*The Raven* by Edgar Allan Poe). These sounds are often described as hissing and include –f (fall), -ch (chin), -th (think), -z (zoo), -x (x-ray) and the soft –c (deceit). It also includes the sound in *measure.*

The difference between **alliteration** and **sibilance** is that alliteration is the repetition of any sound at the beginning of words. Sibilance is the repetition of the above sounds only at the beginning, in the middle or at the end of words.

Simile: A figure of speech in which you compare two things using the words *like* or *as*. For example: *You are like an angel and your eyes are as bright as stars.* There is also a **negative simile**. For example, in Shakespeare's *Sonnet 130*: 'My mistress' eyes are nothing like the sun'.

Symbolism: the use of a symbol to represent an idea or quality. A sunset, for example, symbolises the end of hope or the end of life.

Synecdoche: using part of something to represent the whole of it. For example: *Do you like my new wheels?* In this context, the synecdoche *wheels* means car. **Synecdoche** is similar to **metonymy**, but metonymy uses a more loosely-associated idea. For example, we could admire a new car by saying *it's a nice ride*, but the word *ride* (unlike *wheels*) is not part of a car. Therefore it's a metonym.

Trope: 1. A figure of speech, such as metaphor, hyperbole, irony, litotes, metaphor, oxymoron, etc. 2. A cliché, a device that is overused. For example: *The usual Gothic story tropes.*

Zeugma: using one verb with two or more words to create different meanings. For example: *He broke her heart and her car.*

COMMONLY CONFUSED TERMINOLOGY

Do you know the difference between **mood, tone** and **voice**? Or **narrator** and **persona**? Definitions are below.

Mood: the atmosphere in a piece of writing. Atmosphere is created by the way that the writer describes the setting. For example, in *The Signal-man* by Charles Dickens, the railway cutting is described as: 'a dripping-wet wall of jagged stone, excluding all view but a strip of sky...' This creates an atmosphere or mood of fear and unease. A wet, dripping wall is unappealing to the senses, and the stone is 'jagged', connoting harshness and pain, creating a mood of being under threat. At the bottom of the cutting, all you can see is 'a strip of a sky', evoking a feeling of being trapped, as the reader has the impression of being buried alive.

When you study a text, examine how the mood changes. Tone can also change within a text.

Tone: the writer's attitude towards the subject and implied audience. For example, in *A Modest Proposal*, the satirist Jonathan Swift uses an ironic, contemptuous tone when he suggests that Irish children are cooked and eaten in order to reduce the population: 'a young healthy child well nursed, is, at a year old, a most delicious nourishing and wholesome food, whether stewed, roasted, baked, or boiled'. Obviously, cannibalism is illegal and immoral, so the reader knows that he does not mean what he says. The underlying tone is one of contempt for politicians and the hypocrisy of the wealthy, who have the means to help the poor but do nothing about it.

Voice: while *tone* is specific and will usually change within a text, **voice** is more general and refers to a writer's personality, style and attitude towards the world. Sylvia Plath (1932-1963) was an American novelist and poet, who suffered from depression and finally committed suicide. This helps us understand her voice, which might be called that of a victimised daughter, wife and mother.

Narrator: You can also have a **narrator's voice** in a text. If a story is narrated in the first person, examine how the narrator speaks and thinks.

Sometimes, the narrator might be absent, especially if the narrative is in the third person. Consider the effect that **narrative stance** has on the reader. For example, the benefit of **first person** narration is that you have access to the thoughts and feelings of the narrator; however, the reader only knows what the narrator knows, and this is a disadvantage if significant events are taking place elsewhere. With the **third person** narrative stance, the narrator is omniscient and has access to all the facts, but the reader might be slightly more distanced from the protagonist.

Persona: If the text is fiction or poetry, the narrator might assume another person's identity, and this is called a **persona**.

MISCELLANEOUS TERMINOLOGY

Some useful generic vocabulary follows:

Ambiguity: a word or phrase that is **ambiguous** has more than one meaning. For example: *I saw her duck.* This might mean that I saw her with a bird or I saw her in the act of ducking.

Antagonist: a character who struggles against, competes with, or is opposed to another.

Archetype: a typical example of a person or thing; *he is the **archetypal** hero.*

Auditory language: sound words; for example, anything onomatopoeic.

Catalyst: a person who changes things by speeding up or bringing about an event. The catalyst usually remains unchanged.

Characterisation: how a character is presented. This might be through speech, actions and appearances.

Conflict: a struggle between opposing forces in a play or prose. There can be **internal conflict** that takes place within a character as well as **external conflict**, which is a struggle between other characters and outside forces.

Connotation: the feelings or ideas that a word evokes, different from its literal meaning. For example, the word *angel* **connotes** harps, fluffy clouds, white dresses and goodness.

Convention: a feature of a literary work that you would expect to see. For example, you would expect to see the convention of a happy ending and at least one marriage in a Shakespearean comedy.

Denotation: The dictionary definition of a word.

Lexis: words. A **lexical set** is a group of words that share a similar feature. This might be a similar topic (for example, animal words, words to describe the cold, words to describe the landscape) or function, such as adjectives, nouns, etc.

Gustatory language: words to do with taste.

Olfactory language: words to do with smell.

Parody: a humorous imitation of a person or a literary work.

Pathos: something that makes the audience or reader feel sorry for a character. Some charities use pathos in their advertising when they depict images of starving, impoverished or neglected children.

Plot: the main events in a play, novel, film, etc.

Protagonist: the main character of a play or story.

Register: the type of words that are used for a particular setting. For example: a formal register *(Good morning!)* and an informal register *(Hi!).*

Subplot: a secondary or subordinate plot in a play, novel, film, etc.

Tactile language: words to do with touch.

Tragic flaw: a weakness in a character that leads to his or her downfall.

Tragic hero: a character who makes an error or judgement; this *tragic flaw* leads to his or her downfall.

Visual language: words to do with sight.

Example Analytical Paragraph that Employs Language Terminology

AO2 requires you to use terminology when you explore how meanings are shaped. Read the stanza from *First Love* by John Clare and then study the example analysis overleaf. Terminology is highlighted **bold**.

'FIRST LOVE' by John Clare

I ne'er was struck before that hour

With love so sudden and so sweet,

Her face it bloomed like a sweet flower

And stole my heart away complete.

My face turned pale as deadly pale,

My legs refused to walk away,

And when she looked, what could I ail?

My life and all seemed turned to clay.

Example Analysis:

Clare introduces a bitter-sweet aspect to love with his **metaphor** of being 'struck' by 'love'. The **past participle** 'struck' evokes violence. This is more than being hit by Cupid's arrow, as it has **connotations** of being struck by a sledgehammer, the pain of which is heightened through the use of the **passive voice**: Clare has no power to control the strength of his feelings which are simultaneously pleasurable yet debilitating. This idea is developed in the **stanza** with the death **imagery** of his face turning 'pale as deadly pale' and the **rhetorical question** with 'what could I ail?' to emphasise his reaction 'when she looked'. The physical impact that love at first sight has on Clare can also be seen through the **personification** of his 'legs', which 'refused to walk away'. He has no control over his body at all, and this emphasises the power of the young woman and the strength of his feelings towards her.

Not everything about love is negative, however. The **alliteration** with 's̲o s̲udden and s̲o s̲weet' creates a gentle, almost nostalgic **tone** and emphasises the **adjective** 'sweet', which is repeated in the next line with the **simile** of her 'face' blooming 'like a sweet flower'. The **adjective** 'sweet' **connotes** her beauty might also be from within, as she may have a sweet nature. In addition, the **noun** 'flower' is an **image** drawn from nature, suggesting that it is the most natural thing in the world for this woman to be loved. This nature **imagery** is extended with the **verb** 'bloomed', **connoting** youth and suggesting that she is on the brink of adulthood. The phrase 'life and all seemed turned to clay' is another **image** to do with nature. Clay is malleable and this might **symbolise** that he is so much in love with her, that he will bend his will to do anything that she wants.

However, the clay, coupled with 'deadly pale' also has **connotations** of the grave, suggesting that Clare's old life is now dead. This might be something to mourn, but it can also be interpreted in a positive way. Clay can be shaped into new forms; in the Bible, when God created Adam, he 'formed the man of dust from the ground' (Gen. 2:8). This could therefore **symbolise** how Clare's life has been transformed in a completely new way by the power of his 'first love'.

To Conclude

The above example seamlessly integrates terminology into an analysis, and this is what you should be aiming to do. If you just identify terminology without analysing its usage, this is called *feature spotting*. Avoid this at all costs.

In this chapter, we have focused on terminology for analysing language. In the next chapter, we will review and extend your knowledge of the terminology of structure and form.

Chapter 4

AO1: Structure, Form and Language continued

We have just reviewed some general language terminology, but what's the difference between structure, form and language? This is a question that many students ask and, to add to the confusion, some literary devices overlap.

> **IMPORTANT! A reminder that this guide aims to be a <u>reference</u> book: you're not expected to memorise everything! Your teacher should advise you on which terminology is the most relevant for the particular text that you are studying.**

Form

Imagine a building. There are many types of buildings: for example, a school, fire station and hospital. They are all built for a specific purpose, and you know what they are without having to enter them.

Likewise, the **form** of a text is the first thing we know without having to read it. In the same way that you see immediately that a hospital is a hospital, you can pick up a poem and see that it's a poem.

Form is therefore the way that we classify writing which, like a building, has a distinctive structure or framework.

The main literary forms are drama, essay, novel, novella, poetry, prose and short story. These forms might also split into **sub-forms** just as a business centre might contain floors belonging to different businesses. Examples include:

Prose: fiction, nonfiction

Drama: one-act play, three-act play, five-act play

Poetry: ballad, epic, lyric, narrative, ode, sonnet, villanelle

I wouldn't agonise about whether something is a form or sub-form. It's more important to identify a particular form, consider why the writer has selected it, analyse how it furthers the writer's aims, and develop your ideas about its impact on you, the reader.

Some example forms and their defining features follow; be aware that this is not intended to be a definitive list.

PROSE: EXAMPLE FORMS

Prose is a piece of ordinary writing that consists of sentences and paragraphs. Examples of prose form include:

Autobiography: an account of a person's life; for example, *A Child Called It* by Dave Pelzer

Biography: an account of someone's life, written by another person; for example, *Cheryl: My Story* by Cheryl Cole.

Fable: a brief story with a moral, often including animals. The Greek Aesop is still famous for his fables, published today as *Aesop's Fables*.

Essay: a short piece of writing, usually written in school or at university about a particular subject.

Fiction: creative writing.

Graphic fiction: fictional writing employing dialogue and artwork; for example, comics.

Heroic prose: legends and tales are examples of heroic prose, which are stories that are written down or recited. Heroic prose employs formulaic expressions found in the oral tradition; for example, 'once upon a time'. A famous example of heroic prose is *Gods and Fighting Men* by Lady Gregory.

Nonfiction: narrative prose that is based on facts and reality. Examples include biographies, autobiographies, articles, essays, diaries, blogs and travel writing.

Novel: a long piece of creative writing that tells a story **(fictional prose narrative)**. It can be 50,000 words long or more. Because of its length, there is scope for complex characterisation, plots and subplots.

Novella: a fictional prose narrative, which is shorter than a novel and longer than a short story. It contains roughly 20,000 - 50,000 words. Because of its length, it's less likely to have subplots and multiple narrators. However, descriptions of character and settings are more detailed than in a short story. A famous example of a novella is *Of Mice and Men* by John Steinbeck.

Short story: a fictional prose narrative, which is shorter than a novella. Because it is so short, there are fewer main characters (sometimes there might only be one) and the story will probably contain one major **conflict** (see *structure*, below). One of my favourite short stories is *The Red Room* by H. G. Wells.

DRAMA: EXAMPLE FORMS

Drama is written to be performed on stage, radio or television. Example dramatic forms include:

Five-act play: a play of five acts.

Musical: a play or film with lots of singing and dancing. Songs are interspersed with dialogue.

One-act play: a short play of one act.

Opera: a staged drama that is usually set to classical music with singers and instruments. The singing is usually continuous.

Screenplay: similar to a play, but it contains additional instructions for producing a film, such as camera positions and movement.

Skit: a short satirical or humorous comedy sketch or story.

Three-act play: a play of three acts.

POETRY: EXAMPLE FORMS

Poetry expresses concentrated thoughts and ideas through a distinctive style and rhythm (see *structure*, below). It often rhymes and contains a lot of figurative language (see previous chapter). Example poetic forms include:

Ballad: a poem that tells a story. Historically, it was written to be sung, so it has short stanzas and a repeated **refrain** (see *structure*, below). A popular Victorian example is *The Lady of Shalott* by Alfred Lord Tennyson.

Dramatic monologue: a poem in which there is a distinct persona, who addresses a silent listener. When we read the poem, it is almost as if we are overhearing a speaker in a dramatic situation. You might have studied *My Last Duchess* by Robert Browning, which is a dramatic monologue.

Elegy: a sad poem (or song) that laments the loss of someone who has died.

Epic: a long, serious narrative poem about a significant event and featuring a hero; for example, *The Iliad* or *The Odyssey*, both written by Homer.

Heroic poem: see **epic poem**. There's also **mock-heroic** poetry in which the elevated language from epic poetry is used to describe everyday events or people. The aim is mockery or satire, for example with Alexander Pope's the *Rape of the Lock*.

Haiku: a Japanese poem with three unrhymed lines of five, seven and five syllables.

Idyll: a short poem that describes a rural or pastoral scene. It has a mood of peacefulness and contentment. The modern use of the word 'idyllic' to describe any beautiful or peaceful setting is a good way to remember 'idyll'. Events are set against an idyllic backdrop. Milton's *Lycidas* is an idyll.

Lay: a lyrical, narrative poem often sung by medieval minstrels. Common themes include adventure and romance. An example included *The Lay of the Last Minstrel* by Sir Walter Scott.

Limerick: a light-hearted and humorous poem of five lines and an aabba rhyme scheme. Edward Lear published *Book of Nonsense* in 1846, which contained limericks. An example is:

> There was an old man whose despair
>
> Induced him to purchase a hare:
>
> Whereon one fine day,
>
> He rode wholly away,
>
> Which partly assuaged his despair.

Lyric poem: an emotional poem that expresses the thoughts and feelings of the poet. It does not tell a story. Sonnets and odes are also lyric poems. Nowadays, 'lyrics' often apply to words in a song.

Narrative poem: a poem that tells a story. Epic poems, ballads, idylls and lays are all examples of narrative poems.

Ode: a formal lyric poem, which praises a person, animal, object or event. It's written in an elevated style; for example, *Ode to a Grecian Urn* by John Keats.

Pastoral: a poem about the simplicity and sweetness of rural life, usually containing shepherds or shepherdesses; for example, Christopher Marlowe's *The Passionate Shepherd to his Love*.

Satire: any writing that ridicules the vices, silliness and shortcomings of people, organisations, government or society. Jonathan Swift's *A Beautiful Young Nymph Going to Bed* satirises the bedtime routine of a prostitute.

Sonnet: a fourteen-line poem, usually about love, in iambic pentameter. There is the **Shakespearean sonnet** with a rhyme scheme of ababcdcdefefgg. The three quatrains form an argument, and there is a turn or reversal in the argument called a **volta**. This is often introduced with the words 'but' and 'yet'. This is usually—but not always—at the end of the third quatrain. The rhyming couplet at the end often summarises the argument in the poem or makes a statement about the theme of the poem. The **Petrarchan sonnet** predates the Shakespearean sonnet and it comprises an octave and a sestet. The rhyme scheme of the octave is often abbaabba and either cdecde or another rhyme scheme with the sestet. The **volta** is usually after the octave.

Villanelle: a lyric poem of 19 lines, which has two rhymes and two repeating rhymes. The first and third lines alternate throughout the poem, which is structured in five **tercets** and a **quatrain** (see *structure*, below). *Do Not Go Gentle into that Good Night* by Dylan Thomas is an example of a villanelle.

SO WHAT'S THE DIFFERENCE BETWEEN FORM AND GENRE?

Genre is a **category** of literature, and each **genre shares common literary techniques** such as similarities in tone, plot, themes, settings and characters. To illustrate the difference between form and genre, think of a Gothic novel: 'novel'; is the form and 'Gothic' is the genre.

Genres that have arisen out of particular literary movements will be discussed in chapter 10.

EXAMPLE ANALYSIS OF FORM

When you analyse form, consider why the writer might have chosen it, how it furthers his or her aims, and the extent to which the writer has succeeded. You might also link your thoughts to the context of the poem and the extent to which it conforms to the conventions of a particular literary movement or genre. This is absolutely fine: a blended approach is preferable as it demonstrates your appreciation of the bigger picture.

The example analysis below is of a stanza from *The Rime of the Ancient Mariner* by Samuel Taylor Coleridge. The parts that are **bold** focus on the poet's choice of form and its impact on his readers.

Example Analysis:

The form of Coleridge's *The Rime of the Ancient Mariner* is so distinctive that **it marks the beginning of the Romantic Movement** in England. **Traditionally,** ballads were popular and written to be sung, but Coleridge **manipulated the ballad form to create an artistic poem,** triggering a revival in the popularity of the ballad. **Rejecting the 'mechanical device[s] of style'** used by neoclassical poets, he abandoned fashionable conventions in favour of **'the real language of men'** (1800 Preface). The focus was **now on imaginative creativity and expression.**

Although Coleridge followed convention by using quatrains, he refused to be constrained and he **lengthened key stanzas to emphasise pivotal moments;** for example, the drama of the storm-tossed ship is described in a sestet, thereby lengthening the terror. Moreover, to give the narrative greater authenticity, **Coleridge purposefully imitated an 'archaic' ballad form** with archaic spelling ('Mariner', for example, was originally spelt 'Marinere'), but this was **not well received by contemporary readers, who struggled to understand the poem.** At this point, it is interesting to note that **Coleridge's choice of form contradicts his earlier comment about poetry being written in 'the real language of men'.**

In response to its critical reception, Coleridge adapted the form for the second edition of *Lyrical Ballads* by removing some of the archaic spelling. He also added a Latin epigraph and the structural feature of glosses, which interpret the poem for the reader and aim to provide fake sense of authenticity to the work. Unfortunately, contemporary readers were still not enamoured with the poem, as it was considerably longer than traditional ballads.

COMMMENTARY

The analysis focuses on Coleridge's choice of form and the extent to which it conforms or does not conform to the conventions of the ballad genre. It also discusses Coleridge's choices of language, structure and form in the light of the earlier neoclassical literary movement and the new Romantic Movement. Finally, the analysis reflects on the changes that Coleridge made to the poem because his decision to imitate an archaic ballad form was not well received by contemporary readers. We also see how the length of the ballad had an impact upon its critical reception.

Structure

Let's return to our metaphor of a building. This time, we'll zoom in on a house. Think of all the rooms that it contains: the kitchen and the purpose it serves, the bedroom, the bathroom, the living room and so on. Each room is laid out in a particular way and, when you enter the house, you should bear in mind that it has been designed for you to walk into a particular room first, second, etc. These are the structural features: the way the house is constructed.

In a similar way, **structure** in literary texts is about how the writer deliberately manipulates the reader into thinking about the characters, events and themes in a particular way.

Many of the following structural features apply to prose, drama and poetry, but the rules are not universal.

Length of sentences: long ones for description and short ones to emphasise important moments.

Punctuation for impact. An example is the colon, which is like a trumpet heralding something important in the next clause.

How is **time** manipulated? Explore...

> **Chronology:** is the structure **linear**? In other words, are events described in the order in which they occur? Does the story have an **open structure**? Is the reader (or audience) left to make sense of the ending? Is there a **closed structure**? This means that there is a definite ending (although it might be open to interpretation!). Is the structure **circular** or **cyclical**? In *Of Mice and Men,* for example, the characters end in the same place or **setting** as they began. Broadly speaking, this symbolises that the itinerant workers are not able to change their lives.

Flashbacks: do events from an earlier time occur in the main sequence of events? Why are these flashbacks included?

Foreshadowing: are there hints about future events? These are often seen through symbolism.

Do events take place over a day? A week? Generations, etc.?

How the **narrative point of view** is manipulated. Is the text written in the first, second or third person? Is there a single narrator or are there multiple narrators?

Any **repetition** of words, categories of words, motifs (dominant or recurring ideas) or themes.

The **rhythm of words** in a sentence: most people think that only poetry contains rhythm, but prose and drama contain it as well. In the example 'How I writhed, and yawned, and nodded and, revived!' we can imagine the narrator in Emily Brontë's *Wuthering Heights* restlessly turning in bed, trying to get to sleep.

The **juxtaposition** (placing) of two or more ideas, places, characters or actions next to each other to create a contrast.

Characterisation: is there a foil, a character who contrasts with the main character in a play or story, or whose life parallels that of the main character? Examine decisions to describe a character in an **implicit** (suggested but not directly described) or **explicit** (directly described) fashion. What effect does this create? Has the writer also decided to **withhold important information** about a character from the reader? Why might this be? For example, Austen in *Pride and Prejudice* withholds important information about Mr Wickham's past. Towards the end of the novel, this information is revealed and helps us to understand Mr Darcy's attitude towards him. Moreover, because Mr Wickham's past is a secret, the reader and characters in the book are lulled into a false sense of security, which makes Wickham's elopement with Lydia an unexpected shock.

Use of plot and subplot(s): a subplot is a less important plot. Is it also used as a foil to the main plot?

STRUCTURAL FEATURES OF PROSE

The following structural features are more common in prose texts, but some apply to other genres.

Paragraphs: like sentences, these might vary in length. Consider the impact that this has on the reader.

Chapters: how do they progress the text as a whole? Do they, for example, end on a cliff-hanger or complete a topic?

Headings or subheadings: in nonfiction forms such as reports, these are useful to signpost a thread of discussion. In fiction writing, they might be used as a hook and draw you into a story. Sometimes, chapter headings contain **epigraphs**, short quotations that introduce a theme.

Graphics: the extent to which they are in a text will depend on the purpose of the writing and its form. Younger readers would enjoy looking at the supporting pictures of a story; adults reading nonfiction scientific articles might welcome explanatory charts and diagrams.

Dialogue: how is it written on the page? Look for...

Direct speech: *Se said, "I heard something!"*

Free direct speech looks like direct speech but isn't introduced and doesn't have speech marks. For example: *She entered the house, stopped and listened. I heard something! It's going to get me! She fled.* The shift in narrative to free direct speech puts you inside the character's head and heightens the tension.

Indirect speech, also called **reported speech**, as the speaker

reports something that happened in the past. For example: *She thought what if they stared at her?*

Free indirect speech looks like indirect speech but isn't introduced. For example: *She nervously stood in the doorway. What if they stared at her? She'd be an idiot and trip over her long dress! She must pull herself together! With an air of apparent confidence, she entered the room.*

The final example also begins in the past tense, but the underlined sentences switch to free indirect speech, with no 'she thought' at the beginning. This creates the impression of eavesdropping on the character's thoughts and is another device to develop drama and heighten atmosphere.

STRUCTURAL FEATURES OF DRAMA

Drama texts will contain some or all of the structural features below, depending on when they were written. Shakespeare, for example, has the famous 'Exit, pursued by a bear' stage direction in *The Winter's Tale* but, unlike most modern plays, his stage directions are often embedded into the dialogue.

Acts and scenes: scenes are sub-sections of acts.

Aside: a brief remark, made by a character. The aside reveals his or her thoughts and feelings to the audience. Any other characters on the stage do not 'hear'.

Chorus: in Greek tragedy, a group of characters, who comment on what is happening in a play.

Comic relief: the use of a witty character, humorous dialogue or a comic scene to relieve tension in a serious play.

Dialogue: conversation between characters.

Diction: the way that a character speaks. Examine how words are enunciated and also what the choice of words reveals about character, thoughts, feelings, attitudes and personal values.

List of characters: this helps the director to allocate roles.

Monologue: a long speech, spoken by one character to other characters on stage—not to the audience.

Script: contains dialogue.

Stage directions: usually include information about how an actor might speak, particular mannerisms to employ, what to wear, how to use props, and instructions for entrances and exits. They also cover technical aspects such as how the stage is set, lighting and sound effects.

Soliloquy: a long speech in which a character expresses his or her thoughts to the audience.

STRUCTURAL FEATURES OF POETRY

Stanzas

The poetic equivalent of a paragraph is a **verse** or **stanza**. Here is the terminology for the different stanza lengths and their names:

Couplet: two lines of verse. If the lines rhyme, they're called a **rhyming couplet**. If the couplet is in iambic pentameter, it's a **heroic couplet**.

Tercet: a stanza of three lines that often rhymes. If the rhyme scheme is aaa, it's a **triplet**.

Quatrain: a stanza of four lines. There are four types of rhymed quatrains: the **cross-rhyme** abab; the **envelope-rhyme** abba; the **rhyming couplets** aabb; and the **monorhyme** aaaa.

Quintain: a stanza or poem of five lines. Limericks are quintains.

Sestet: a group of six lines of poetry, most often found in the second half of a Petrarchan sonnet.

Septet: a stanza of seven lines

Octave: a stanza (verse) of eight lines, often found in the first half of a Petrarchan sonnet.

Structural Features Relating to Language

Some of the following features apply to a range of genres; others to poetry only. They should be self-evident when you read them.

Anaphora: Repetition of the same word or words at the beginning of sentences. For example, the word 'this' in:

> This blessed plot, this earth, this realm, this England,
> This nurse, this teeming womb of royal kings . . .
> This land of such dear souls, this dear, dear land.

— Richard II by William Shakespeare

Apostrophe: We all know that this is a punctuation mark, but did you know that it's also a word to describe a sudden address to an inanimate object or someone who is either dead or simply not there? For example:

O rose thou art sick.

— *The Sick Rose* by William Blake

Blank verse: the same as iambic pentameter (see below), but iambic pentameter rhymes and blank verse does not.

Caesura (plural caesurae): a significant pause within a line of poetry, usually shown by a full stop, colon, semi-colon, ellipsis or dash.

Elision: Leaving parts out of a word. An apostrophe shows where the letters have been missed out. For example, Shakespeare uses:

Elision	Full word(s)
'tis	It is
Ne'er	never
Ha'	have

Enjambment (also spelt enjambement): in poetry, this is when a line carries over into the next line or even into the next stanza. Here's an example from Edmund Spenser's Sonnet 75 from 'Amoretti':

One day I wrote her name upon the strand,

But came the waves and washed it away:

Again I wrote it with a second hand,

But came the tide, and made my pains his prey.

When quoting an example of enjambment, use a forward slash to show where the line ends on the poem. For example: 'One day I wrote her name upon the strand,/But came the waves and washed it away'.

End-stop: a full stop at the end of a line of poetry.

Feminine rhyme: a rhyme of stressed syllables followed by one or more unstressed syllable. For example, Ben Johnson in *Those Eyes* uses feminine rhyme with 'seeing' and 'being':

> Ah! do not wanton with those eyes,
>
> Lest I be sick with seeing;
>
> Nor cast them down, but let them rise,
>
> Lest shame destroy their being.

Free verse: poetry with no pattern in line length, metre and rhyme.

Hypermetrical: where a line of verse has an extra syllable. For example, in Shakespeare's *Hamlet*, there are eleven instead of ten syllables in the famous line:

x / x / x / / x x / x

To be, | or not | to be: | that is the | question

Monorhyme: A rhyme scheme in which all the lines have the same rhyme.

Plosive: The sounds 'p', 'b', 't' and 'd'. Think of them exploding out of your mouth— consider how the plosive consonants affect the writer's tone.

Polysyndeton: the multiple use of conjunctions. For example: The empty house is quiet and cold and sad and old.

Refrain: In poetry, this is a repeated line or phrase at regular intervals. In music, it's a chorus.

Rhyme: words with an identical or similar vowel sound, followed by an identical or similar consonant sound (for example: *cup, pup*). With **eye rhyme**, the vowels and final consonants look as if they should rhyme but they do not (*good, food*). **Internal rhyme** is where a word in the middle of a line rhymes with a word at the end of a line or within a different line. **Masculine rhyme** is rhyme between stressed syllables at the end of a line of poetry (*stop, pop,* or *complain, refrain*) as opposed to rhyme between unstressed syllables at the end of a line of poetry (see **feminine rhyme,** above).

Rhyme scheme: a regular pattern of rhyme within a stanza or poem. To determine the rhyme scheme of a poem, look at the last syllable of the word at the end of the first line. In the example poem below, it's 'wood'. Now label it with the letter 'a'. Next, study the last syllable of line two. In our example, 'me' does not rhyme with 'wood' so we label it with the letter 'b'. At the end of the third line, we see that 'good' rhymes with 'wood' so we label it 'a'. Continue until you reach the end of the stanza.

> I walk in loneliness through the greenwood
>
> For I have none to go with me.
> Since I have lost my friend by not being good
> I walk in loneliness through the greenwood.
> I'll send him word and make it understood
> That I will be good company.
> I walk in loneliness through the greenwood
> For I have none to go with me.

The rhyme scheme of this poem, written by an anonymous woman in the 12th century, is abaaabab.

Rhythm: the pattern of stressed and unstressed syllables in verse or prose. The rest of this chapter explains these patterns.

Stanza: a formal word for verse.

Syllable: a unit of sound. For example, *exercising* has four syllables, *impressionable* has five and *supercalifragilisticexpialidocious* has 14. A word with one syllable (*bang*) is **monosyllabic** while a word with more than one syllable is **polysyllabic**.

Volta: a turn in argument in a sonnet.

Structural Features of Feet

A **foot** is a unit (or set) of stressed and unstressed syllables. The most common ones in English poetry are listed below, but there are more. In the examples below, each stressed syllable is marked.

Name of Foot	Sounds like...	Example
Iamb	di dúm	a cát
Trochee	dúm di	Naughty

Spondee	dúm dúm	Hosepipe
Anapest (or anapaest)	di di dúm	in the town
Dactyl	dúm di di	Fabulous

Structural Features of Meter

The pattern of feet in a line is called **meter**. For example:

A line of...	Is called...	Because the prefix comes from the...
One foot	monometer	Greek word *mónos*, which means alone.
Two feet	dimeter	Greek word *dis*, which means twice.
Three feet	trimeter	Greek word *tri,* which means three.
Four feet	tetrameter	Greek word *tetra*, which means four.
Five feet	pentameter	Greek word *penta*, which means five.
Six feet	hexameter	Greek word *hexa*, which means six.
Seven feet	heptameter	Greek word *hepta*, which means seven.
Eight feet	octameter	Greek word *octa*, which means eight.

The next step is to combine feet with meter. In the examples below:

- The stressed syllables are marked with /
- The unstressed syllables are marked with x
- The feet have been marked off with vertical lines (this is a useful way of working out the metre)

Combining Feet with Meter

Iambic pentameter: five iambic metrical feet per line. In other words, ten syllables f alternating unstressed and stressed syllables per line.

x   /   x   /   x   /   x   /   x   /

My mist | ress' eyes | are noth | ing like | the sun

—*Sonnet 130* by William Shakespeare

Iambic tetrameter: four iambic feet per line.

   x   /   x   /   x /   x   /

Had we | but world | enough | and time,

—*To his Coy Mistress* by Andrew Marvell

Iambic trimeter: three iambic feet per line.

   x   /   x /   x   /

I love | the jo | cund dance

   x   /   x   /   x   /

The soft | ly breath | ing song

—*Song* by William Blake

Trochaic pentameter: five trochaic feet per line. For example:

   /   x   /   x   /   x   /   x   /   x

Nev | er, nev | er, nev |er, nev | er, nev | er!

— *King Lear* by William Shakespeare

Trochaic tetrameter: a line of four trochaic feet. For example:

   /   x   / x   / x   / x

With the | odors | of the | forest,

   /   x   /   x   /   x   /   x

With the | dew and | damp of | meadows

—*The Song of Hiawatha* by Henry Wadsworth Longfellow (NB: American spelling of 'odours')

Anapestic tetrameter: four anapestic feet per line. For example:

x x / x x / x x / x x /

And the sheen | of their spears | was like stars | on the sea

—*The Destruction of Sennacherib* by Lord Byron

Dactylic hexameter: a line of six dactyls. For example:

/ x x / x x / x x / x x / x x / x

This is the | forest prim | eval, the | murmuring | pine and the | hemlocks

— *Evangeline* by Henry Wadsworth Longfellow

Trochaic monometer: it's rare to find a poem that's written in this metre. There is a famous poem called *Fleas* by Ogden Nash that's written in trochaic monometer, and some people say is the shortest poem in the world. Can you guess the words and then find the poem online?

Variations in Meter

You might have noticed in the *Evangeline* example that Longfellow has used 17 instead of 18 syllables in the line, replacing the last dactyl with a trochee.

Poets do not always stick to the metrical pattern, and their poems would be extremely predictable if they did. Watch out for dropped syllables, extra syllables and changes in the meter. This is a deliberate device to emphasise words and convey a particular mood or voice.

Poets can also combine meters. For example, *The Rime of the Ancient Mariner* contains a loose meter with the even lines being generally iambic trimeter and the odd lines being generally iambic tetrameter:

x / x / x / x /

The ice | was here, | the ice | was there,

x / x / x /

The ice | was all | around:

x / x / x / x /

It cracked | and growled, | and roared | and howled,

x / x / x /

Like nois | es in | a swound!

It's rare to find a poem that's only written in spondees, which is why I haven't given any examples so far. A spondee is usually inserted to make another type of metrical foot irregular. For example:

/ / / / x / x / x /

Cry, cry! | Troy burns, | or else | let Hel | en go.

— *Troilus and Cressida* by William Shakespeare

As we can see in the above example, emotion can create a spondee. Emotion can also create a trochee; study the first two syllables of *Holy Sonnet 14* by John Donne, which is written in iambic pentameter:

/ x x / x / x / x /

Batter | my heart, | three-pers |on'd God, |for you

38

Perhaps a simpler way of talking about a stress change when the rest of the line is in iambic pentameter is to say that there is **inverted stress** with 'batter' or that Donne uses an **inversion**. Then analyse it! Not sure how to do this? Read on.

EXAMPLE ANALYSIS OF STRUCTURE

Being able to identify iambic pentameter, trochees, spondees and so on is all very well, but how do you write about them in an essay?

You will probably blend language analysis into your analysis of structure because meter deliberately emphasises particular words.

Below is an example analysis of the structure of a stanza from *The Rime of the Ancient Mariner*. To put the analysis in context, up until this point in the poem, Coleridge has conformed to the structural conventions of ballads: he has employed quatrains with either abcb or abab rhyme schemes. Although there are exceptions, the first and third lines are iambic tetrameter while the second and fourth lines are in trimeter.

Read the following stanza and then study the analysis:

> With sloping masts and dipping prow,
>
> As who pursued with yell and blow
>
> Still treads the shadow of his foe,
>
> And forward bends his head,
>
> The ship drove fast, loud roar'd the blast,
>
> And southward aye we fled.

Terminology and analysis that link to structure have been highlighted in **bold.**

Example Analysis:

Coleridge's readers, who are used to the traditional **quatrains** of ballads, might be surprised and shocked to encounter a **sestet**. Its length and use of enjambment **evoke a feeling of never-ending horror** for the terrified sailors, who are recklessly pursued by the storm. A feeling of panic and chaos is developed through the fast pace of the **iambic tetrameter in the first three lines**. The **stresses** on 'sloping masts' and 'dipping prow' **emphasise** the idea that the ship will go down and all hands will be lost. The **stresses** on the onomatopoeic nouns 'yell' and 'blow' also emphasise the violence of the storm. Moreover, the **stress** on 'foe' **underpins** the storm's malicious intent. Therefore, the regular meter of **iambic tetrameter creates** a mood of relentless determination of the storm to catch the sailors.

This mood changes in the fourth line with the switch to **iambic trimeter** with:

     x   /   x   /   x   /

     And for | ward bends | his head

Continued…

There is now a **change in tone** as the personified ship demonstrates a new-found determination to outrun the storm. Then the **meter** changes again:

     x   /   x   /   / /   x   /

     The ship | drove fast, | loud roar'd | the blast

The **spondee** with 'loud roar'd' **emphasises** the rage of the storm as the ship escapes. The onomatopoeic 'roar'd' also **connotes** the idea of a predator losing its prey.

With the return to **regular iambic trimeter** in the final line of the stanza ('And southward aye we fled'), the stress on the positive 'aye' **marks** a feeling of relief. The **last** word of the stanza is 'fled', which also **emphasises** safety. It is no coincidence that the stanza that follows returns to the reassuring and familiar form of a **quatrain**.

COMMENTARY

Obviously, you would not be analysing a complete poem in so much detail. In order to focus your thoughts, you should carefully read the set question, making a careful note of the key words. Then write about the parts of the poem that are the most relevant to the question.

You now have an example of how to blend references to meter into your writing as well as how to quote a line and analyse variations in meter. It's worth repeating that you should focus on the impact of the words that the meter emphasises.

Before we finish this chapter, here is an optional activity that you might enjoy.

Test Yourself!

Samuel Taylor Coleridge once wrote a mnemonic poem called *Metrical Feet* to help his son to identify examples of each type of foot. Can you mark the stresses and feet?

1. *Metrical Feet – wheres thae answer?*

2. Trochee trips from long to short

3. From long to long in solemn sort

4. Slow spondee stalks; strong foot yet ill able

5. Ever to come up with dactyl trisyllable.

6. Iambics march from short to long.

7. With a leap and a bound the swift anapests throng.

ANSWER

1. / x   /   x   /   x   /

    Trochee | trips from |long to | short

2.   x   /   x /   x /   x   /

    From long | to long | in sol | emn sort

3. /   / /   /   /   / /   / x

    Slow spond | ee stalks; | strong foot | yet ill | able

4. / x x   /   x   x   /   x   x   / x x

    Ever to | come up with | dactyl tri | syllable.

5. x /   x   /   x   /   x   /

    Iam | bics march | from short | to long.

6. x x /   x x /   x   x   /   x x   /

    With a leap | and a bound | the swift an | apests throng.

Summary

If **form** is a type of building and **structure** is the way that the rooms are arranged, **language** can be represented by the contents of a room. A kitchen, for example, contains dozens of different things that have different purposes: saucepans, cutlery, a kettle and cups.

All of the elements of form, structure and language combine to create meaning. Your task is to consider why the writer has chosen to employ them and their impact on the reader.

AO1 also assesses your ability to express yourself in a coherent, accurate way. This is the topic of the next chapter.

Chapter 5

AO1: Coherent, Accurate Written Expression

A reminder that Assessment Objective 1 requires you to:

Articulate informed, personal and creative responses to literary texts, using associated concepts and terminology, and coherent, accurate written expression.

This chapter will focus on 'coherent, accurate written expression' by reviewing useful phrases to develop your writing style and explore layers of meaning. This will increase your chances of accessing higher grades. We'll then review planning and how to organise your ideas into a logical, persuasive argument.

Coherent, accurate written expression means that you should express yourself in a clear, concise way, using formal English. This involves writing words in full (*he is* instead of *he's*, for example). You must also use formal vocabulary—no slang!

It goes without saying that your spelling, punctuation and grammar should be of the highest possible standard. If you need to do some revision, I make no apology for recommending *Mr Bruff's Guide to Grammar*, which is aimed at GCSE students and provides an excellent foundation for A' level. It is available both on Amazon ow.ly/3v2v8P and on Mr Bruff's website http://mrbruff.com/product/mr-bruffs-guide-to-grammar-ebook/ at a lower price.

If there are particular words that you misspell, you might want to consider creating a **personal spelling list** of the corrected words to learn.

Likewise, review work that your teacher returns to you. Learn the corrections of errors in grammar and vocabulary, asking your teacher if you don't understand.

Useful Phrases

The following phrases encourage you to express yourself with fluency. They also help you to drill beneath the surface of a text to explore layers of meaning. They have been contextualised in example sentences so that you can see how they are used. Try experimenting with them in your next analysis.

Some readers might propose that the protagonist cares a lot about others; **other readers might argue that** she only helps others when the media are watching.

At first glance, it appears that a swallow is flying out of the window**; however,** the swallow might symbolise the woman's journey to the afterlife as she moves from this world to the next.

Despite the initial impression of beauty in the garden, the fact that the flowers are 'wilting' implies that the owner of the garden is no longer at the peak of health.

Although on the surface it may seem that the man is friendly, the animal imagery with 'bared his teeth' and 'howled with laughter' has undercurrents of violence.

Whilst some readers might feel this is a book about a zoo, **it is clear that** the zoo is a metaphor for the world in which we live.

Useful Verbs

The word 'X'...

> connotes, has connotations of, hints at, depicts, evokes, illustrates, implies, reveals, suggests, symbolises...

Words to Replace 'the Quote...'

It looks rather clumsy to say 'the quote'. Instead, replace this phrase with one of the words below. The...

> announcement, assertion, declaration, exclamation, idea, image, phrase, question, remark, sentence, suggestion...

Quoting

This seems to be an appropriate moment to clarify that your ability to quote is assessed against AO2, which will be reviewed in chapter 7.

Having said this, certain questions on some of the exam papers do not directly assess AO2. In this case, the examiner would credit you for an accurate use of quotations that help either to contextualise a specific point or to contribute to a more coherent argument, in which case, you would be assessed under AO1.

Remember that quotations should be used in a way that is appropriate to the question: use them thoughtfully to support the direction of your argument.

Structuring a Coherent Argument

A coherent argument is well structured and has a clear thread of discussion. AO1 assesses your ability to organise your ideas into a logical, convincing argument with one clear theme per paragraph. The notes below apply to any type of essay, including comparative essays, which will be discussed in more detail in chapter 11.

KEY WORDS

Before you plan an essay, underline the key words of the question to focus your ideas. This might sound obvious, but under the pressure of exam conditions, some students rush, misread the question and therefore gain a low mark because they have not answered it.

PICK APART THE QUESTION

It's worth remembering that examiners prefer you to think independently. They will help you to do this by writing an exam question that invites you to disagree at some point in your response. This provides you with the opportunity to demonstrate your critical skills. The following phrases encourage this:

To what extent...

How far and in what ways do you agree with/that...

Examine...

Explore...

Explain...

Consider...

Consider the view that...

In the light of this comment, discuss...

Write a critical appreciation of...

Discuss the view that...

Explore ways in which...

Explore/discuss the importance of...

Evaluate the view that...

Identify how many parts a question has. For example, in the first part of a question, you might be expected to analyse part of a text closely. In the second part, you might be invited to discuss and interpret a particular aspect of the author's work. Your plan should address the two parts of the question. When you have picked apart the question, try rephrasing it in a couple of sentences. This is a good way of checking that you fully understand it.

PLANNING

Now brainstorm your ideas. Once your thoughts are on paper, number them so that your ideas in your essay progress in a logical way. The most important points should be first. Include a counterargument in your plan to showcase your critical skills.

Everyone has their preferred style of planning; some people use mind maps while others write lists. Whichever method you use, you cannot ignore or rush this stage. If your plan is underdeveloped, it's likely to result in a poorly organised essay, full of waffle and repetition. Your ideas might not be relevant to the question and there will be no clear thread of discussion.

Finally, check that you have covered the relevant assessment objectives. Your teacher should have told you which AOs are being assessed and what percentage of the essay each one is worth. Check that you have covered them in your plan. For example, if relevant, have you used terminology (AO1)? Referenced and responded to the views of others (AO5)? Demonstrated how context (AO3) and analytical methods (AO2) have informed your understanding?

INTRODUCTION

Many students struggle with introductions. At all costs, avoid the clunky and boring: 'In this essay, I am going to discuss...' You need to make an interesting point.

So how do you do this? State your point of view (or hypothesis) in a clear, concise way. This is called a **thesis statement** and it is usually one sentence long. You then spend the rest of the essay justifying (or proving) your thesis statement.

If the exam question starts with a quotation, you could summarise it in your own words and link it to the question. Then follow it with your thesis statement.

EXAMPLE INTRODUCTIONS

Example Introduction 1:

'Blake's poetry explores many facets of love.' How far and in which ways do you agree with this view?

Blake's presentation of the different and sometimes contradictory forms of love will be explored by examining poems from *Selected Poems*. I agree that his poetry explores a great many facets of love, but there are also limitations.

There is a lot of discussion about whether to use the word 'I' in an introduction. If you replace 'I agree that' with 'Many believe that , for example, it sounds more academic. However, some teachers—and even university professors—are happy with the word 'I', as they believe that your opinions are less likely to become lost behind those of others.

Note that this is a very short introduction, but it does focus on the question and have a thesis statement. A more sophisticated way to develop an introduction would be to begin with a relevant quotation. This could be linked to the key words of the question and then lead to a thesis statement.

Example Introduction 2:

Explore the presentation of men and women in 'Pride and Prejudice'.

The subject of men and women is introduced in the first sentence of the Austen's *Pride and Prejudice* with the ironic observation: 'It is a truth universally acknowledged that a single man in possession of a good fortune must be in want of a wife'. This introduces the idea of rational marriage, which is based on economic arrangements. But are all men and women presented in such a mercenary light? I believe that some are, but others are not.

In example 2, we see that an introductory quotation is a good way of introducing one aspect of how men and women are presented. It leads to a pertinent point about marriage and then leads seamlessly to the thesis statement that opens opportunities to cover a wider range of points about relationships and also to disagree with the question.

Another way of structuring an introduction is to contextualise the question by linking it to the background. The thesis statement would then follow.

Example Introduction 3:

Explore the presentation of women in 'Sense and Sensibility'.

In nineteenth century English society, middle and upper class women did not enjoy the same level of education as men, as they were expected to marry and have children. Prevailing attitudes centred on women being weak and not capable of 'rational' thought. This is a view that was challenged by Mary Wollstonecraft in *A Vindication of the Rights of Woman* in 1792. Austen explores contemporary discussions about the nature of women in *Sense and Sensibility*: Elinor Dashwood with her intelligence and practical outlook represents 'sense' and her emotional sister Marianne represents 'sensibility'. This use of antithesis to present women will now be explored.

Whichever method you prefer, remember that a successful introduction is short, establishes basic fact(s) and contains a good thesis statement. This is the foundation for the rest of your essay.

BODY OF ESSAY

Aim to link your topic sentences explicitly to the key words of the question, as this will help to maintain focus. *You* might know how your points connect, but you won't be doing yourself any favours if you expect the examiner to read your mind.

It is worth noting that in the process of writing you might explore points which were not in your plan. This is more likely to be the case if you're writing under pressure in an exam. As long as your points are relevant, this is fine: you don't have to stick to your plan exactly, and the fact that you are developing your thread of discussion or argument through an exploratory approach shows the examiner that you are analysing the text and engaging with it in a personal, creative way.

Always assume the examiner has read the text, so there is no need to narrate the plot. You should focus on quoting and interpreting. This skill is dealt with in more detail in the next chapter.

USEFUL DISCOURSE MARKERS

When you are writing, you need to signpost your ideas so that the examiner can see how your argument is developing. To do this, you need discourse markers. The ones below are useful for developing and extending your thoughts.

Introducing Ideas

To begin with, ...

Primarily, ...

The writer introduces...

We are introduced to...

Developing Ideas

My initial impression is..., but...

My first impression is..., but...

Upon further examination, ...

Upon further consideration, ...

Having considered this, ...

Having considered this point of view, ...

From this, we can see/note/deduce that...

The reader can see/deduce from this that...

It can be seen/said/noted that...

Not only is/are..., but......also…

Sequencing Ideas

The writer then...

Moreover, ...

Furthermore...

In addition, ...

Concluding Ideas

Having considered the evidence, ...

Having considered the evidence that...

Having considered the evidence on both sides, ...

To conclude, ...

In conclusion, ...

It is important to conclude with...

Weighing up the evidence, we can see that...

Finally, ...

Overall, ...

Although these phrases guide your reader through your discussion, try not to overuse them, as you don't want to risk sound artificial. Aim to integrate them seamlessly into your writing.

CONCLUSION

In your conclusion, do not repeat the points that you have already written in the essay. Likewise, do not introduce new material. Instead, reference the exam question, weigh up your thoughts and either confirm your original thesis statement or refine it.

Example Conclusion 1:

'Cleopatra is a manipulative woman, who brings down a worthy soldier and ruler.' To what extent do you agree with this view? Explore the ways that Shakespeare presents Cleopatra.

To conclude, I believe that it is unjust to label Cleopatra as 'manipulative' and to blame her for Anthony's downfall; this would depict her as an unscrupulous schemer, and there is more 'infinite variety' to her character than that. The play is a tragedy, and this choice of genre heightens the downfall of both protagonists, who have to deal with the political consequences of their love. Cleopatra is a woman in love and, although foolish at times, she does not have the malice and scheming ways of Lady Macbeth. As mentioned above, Anthony is not entirely a worthy soldier, having ignored Enobarbus's sound advice to fight on land where he has the advantage. Moreover, Anthony's decision to follow Cleopatra when she panics at the Battle of Actium is what ultimately leads to his downfall. Like Cleopatra, he is not perfect, but he is certainly not a victim of a manipulative schemer

Another way to end a conclusion is to include a quotation that summarises your point of view. This can be a powerful technique if you have an appropriate and relevant quotation to hand.

Example Conclusion 2:

W.B. Yeats commented that 'passive suffering is not a theme for poetry'.

How far do you agree that Owen's poetry is too preoccupied with sentimentalising the soldiers?

Finally, when Yeats sneers at Owen, it is because the former believes that soldiers should be described as tragic heroes rather passive victims. Owen aims to challenge this view and is quick to criticise those who glorify war (*Dulce et Decorum Est*); those who do not understand shellshock (*Mental Cases*) and those who die of exposure in the trenches (*Exposure*). I disagree with Yeats's assessment of Owen's poetry as we all sentimentalise soldiers and I believe that it is our duty to do so. This is seen in the annual remembrance services on 11th November, which help us to remember the sacrifices of the 'doomed youth' from the First World War and the soldiers who fought and died for us in subsequent wars. As Owen states:

'My subject is War, and the pity of War. The Poetry is in the pity'.

Your conclusion might also move beyond the core text(s) to consider wider significant issues.

Example Conclusion 3:

Explore the ways that the character of Scrooge is used to convey Dickens's attitudes towards the poor.

In conclusion, more than 150 years after the novel was first published, the theme of charity in *A Christmas Carol* is still relevant today. As the old saying affirms, 'money cannot buy happiness', and Scrooge learns that it is kindness to others—and the poor in particular—that brings rewards. Dickens stressed the importance of considering others, and perhaps more people in society would benefit today if they took these maxims to heart.

However you structure your conclusion, remember to express yourself concisely. A conclusion summarises your ideas, so it does not have to be very long.

FINAL STAGE OF WRITING AN ESSAY

The final stage of writing is one that many students do not reach: always allow time to check your work. Effective time management is the key and could result in the extra mark that might raise your grade.

An example of a complete essay that contains the features of this chapter is in the bonus chapter at the end of this book.

Chapter 6

AO1: Referencing, Footnotes and Bibliography

If you are doing AS English literature, skip this chapter and save it for the second year of your A' level. Take it to university, though, as it will continue to be useful.

In the second year of your A' level, you have a **non-exam assessment**, which your teacher might call **coursework**. Your teacher will read your draft, give you advice and mark your finished response. It will then be moderated by a member of the English department before being sent to the exam board for external moderation.

In this particular assessment, you are expected to reference your wider reading, use footnotes and write a bibliography.

IMPORTANT! This is an incredibly detailed chapter because it aims to provide you with everything you need to know about how to reference your wider reading.

I recommend that you read the first four pages in detail. Then dip into the middle part of the chapter as and when you need to reference particular media. Resume close reading with 'Multiple Citations' and 'How do I write a Bibliography?' as these are important.

This is an incredibly academic chapter so there are some hidden jokes to lighten it a little. Enjoy! ;)

Important: Plagiarism!

Plagiarism is stealing another person's ideas and passing them off as your own. This is a very serious offence: if you attempt to steal someone's ideas and are caught, you risk being awarded no marks. You might also be barred from sitting one or more exam, for a particular period of time, and not gain your A' level(s).

As you are expected to read widely, you will encounter a range of different interpretations of the texts that you are studying as well as vital contextual information. To avoid accusations of plagiarism, you should acknowledge any wider reading that you quote, paraphrase or describe.

There are lots of different systems for referencing your reading. We're going to focus on the **MHRA (Modern Humanities Research Association) referencing system**, which is in common use at British universities.

MHRA Referencing System

Only reference your wider reading, which we call **secondary sources**. Don't reference the core texts that you have been studying in class, which are your **primary sources**.

When you **cite** (quote or refer to) a secondary source, you need to acknowledge where it came from, but you don't want all the detail that this involves to interrupt the thread of your discussion. After all, your primary aim is to show how your wider reading informs your views—not have it bog you down. This is why we have footnotes: cite your wider reading in your essay and then acknowledge your **source of information** in the footnote.

As you can see in the following example, all quotations must be in single inverted commas (single quotation marks):

Example quotation and footnote:

According to Major and Minor, the protagonist's character was 'profoundly affected by his discordant childhood'.[1]

---

[1]D. Major and A. Minor, *Literary Notes* (London: Chime Publications, 2015), p. 6

To create a footnote, insert a **superscript number** at the end of your sentence (after the full stop). To do this on Word, click the 'References' tab and press the 'Insert Footnote' button. Your superscript number will appear after your citation and again at the bottom of the page, ready for your footnote. Your first footnote is number 1 and the superscript number rises as you add more footnotes.

WHY NOT SIMPLY TYPE THE NUMBER?

The benefit of using a superscript number is that when you make changes to your draft, your footnote automatically moves with your changes. This is very useful if you have a lot of footnotes.

SO WHAT DO I DO NEXT?

The way that you cite your wider reading in your footnotes will vary according to your secondary sources. Examples are provided below.

WHAT IF I'M CITING FROM A BOOK?

If you are citing from a book, write:

1. The author's first name or initial and then his or her surname. After the surname, insert a comma. (If there are three or more authors, write the first author's name and then the words 'and others'.)

2. The title of the book in italics. The main words in the title should be capitalised. The same rule applies to a subtitle if there is one. Introduce any subtitle with a colon.

3. After the title, write the edition number if this information is available.

4. The following information should be inside one set of brackets:

   a. The place of publication. Insert a colon.

   b. The publisher's name. Insert a comma.

   c. The year that the book was published. Close brackets and insert a comma.

   All this information is on the inside cover of your book. If there is a list of publication dates, use the most recent.

5. The page number or the page numbers (a single number is written as p. 6 and a range of page numbers is recorded as pp. 6-12). End with a full stop.

If the reference spills over onto the next line, the second and subsequent lines should be indented.

Example footnote for a book:

[1]Earl Lee Riser, *A New Age Dawns*, 2nd edn (New York: Sunrise Publications, 2014), pp. 83-96.

WHAT IF IT'S A CHAPTER FROM AN EDITED BOOK?

An edited book might contain chapters that are written by different people. If you want to quote from a particular chapter, record the following details in this order:

1. Chapter author(s). Insert comma.

2. Title of chapter (in quotation marks: no italics). Insert comma.

3. The word 'in' followed by the title of book, which is in italics. Insert comma.

4. Add 'ed. by' and the name(s) of the editor(s).

5. Open brackets. Insert place of publication, colon, name of publisher, comma, and year of publication. Close brackets. Insert comma.

6. Insert the chapter's page numbers. Then in brackets write the page(s) you have cited. End with a full stop.

Example footnote for a chapter in an edited book:

[1]Oren Jellow, 'Colours', in *The Rainbow,* ed. by Paige Turner (Paris: Eiffel Books, 2015), pp. 178-263 (p. 201).

WHAT IF IT'S AN EBOOK?

If it's a book that you have downloaded onto your Kindle, iPad or ereader, use the same formula as you would for a printed book. (If some of the information is not available, you will have to leave it out.) At the end, write the type of ereader.

WHAT IF IT'S AN ONLINE EBOOK?

Again, use the same formula as you would for a printed book and use what information is available—if you can't get all the information you need, don't worry. If you're not sure about the place of publication, look for an address and use the location of the publisher's offices. If no page numbers are available, look for numbered paragraphs (record them as, for example, para 3 of 6). Alternatively, you might be able to write a section or chapter number. Insert the name of the database (for example, Project Post) and copy and paste the website's URL. In square brackets, include the date that you accessed the book.

WHAT IF IT'S A WEBSITE ARTICLE?

Use the same formula as you would for an ebook on a database. The only difference is that you might not have the author's name. Instead, replace it with the organisation's name. If there is no information about the organisation, start your reference with the title of the article. If you can't find a date, write [n.d.], which means 'no date'.

WHAT IF IT'S SOMETHING I WATCHED ON YOUTUBE?

Follow the same rules as a website article, but include the type of source after the title. You will also need to include the date it was published, the URL, and the date that you accessed it.

Example footnote for a video from YouTube:

[1]Mr Bruff, *Grammar Tuesday: A* Rhetorical Devices,* online video recording, YouTube, 3 February 2015 https://youtu.be/i5Mxud7yP9Y?list=PLqGFsWf-P-cAs4wAQ9_5izpACHpxM0HN [accessed March 31, 2015].

WHAT IF IT'S A JOURNAL ARTICLE?

1. Author(s). Insert comma.

2. Title of article (in quotation marks: no italics). Insert comma.

3. Title of journal in italics. Insert comma.

4. Volume number.

5. Year of publication in brackets. Insert comma.

6. The page numbers of the article, but don't put pp. in front.

7. Finally, in brackets the page number(s) of citation with p. or pp. in front. End with full stop.

Example footnote for a journal article:

[1]Charity Case, 'The Plight of the Poor', *Philanthropic Journal,* 46 (2015), 58-68 (p. 62).

WHAT IF IT'S AN ONLINE JOURNAL ARTICLE?

If you reference a journal article that you have found online, follow the same format as for a printed journal. The only difference is that you need to add the URL, followed by the date that you accessed the article in square brackets. If page numbers are not available, leave them out. If the paragraphs are numbered, use those instead. If not, leave them out.

Example footnote for a journal article from a website:

[1]K. Spag, 'The Beauty of Grammar', *British Grammar Journal,* 46 (2015), http://www.britishgrammarjournal.co.uk [accessed 31 March 2015] (para 8 of 17).

WHAT IF IT'S A NEWSPAPER OR MAGAZINE ARTICLE?

1. If available, write the journalist's first name or initial and then his or her surname. After the surname, insert a comma. If the journalist's name is not published, begin with the title of the story.

2. The title of the story is in single inverted commas (no italics). Insert comma.

3. Write the name of the newspaper or magazine in italics. (NB: Don't use 'A' or 'The' to introduce your newspaper or magazine unless it's *The Times.*) Insert comma.

4. Write the day, month, year of the article (no punctuation in between). Insert comma.

5. Write the page number(s). End with a full stop.

Example footnote for a newspaper or magazine article:

[1]B. Lowe, 'Underground Caverns', *Twiddleswick News,* 1 April 2015, p. 8.

WHAT IF IT'S A SECTION OF A NEWSPAPER OR MAGAZINE??

If your reference is from a particular section of a newspaper, for example, a travel supplement magazine, include it after the date:

Example footnote for a newspaper or magazine article:

[1]Gail Storm, 'Why the Tempest Calls', *Twiddleswick News,* 1 April 2015, Twiddleswick travel supplement, p. 2.

WHAT IF IT'S AN ONLINE NEWSPAPER OR MAGAZINE ARTICLE?

If you are quoting from an online newspaper article, follow the procedure for a printed newspaper or magazine article, but leave out the page number. Then at the end, add the title of the website's homepage in quotation marks, followed by a comma, the URL of the article, another comma and the date you accessed the article in square brackets. Finish with a full stop.

Example footnote for an online newspaper or magazine article:

[1]Hugh Morris, 'Laugh at Life', *Twiddleswick News,* 1 April 2015, in 'twiddleswick.co.uk', http://www.twiddleswick.co.uk/news/laugh/life, [accessed 31 March 2015].

WHAT IF IT'S A FILM?

For a film, write the title in italics, comma, the name of the director, open bracket, name of the distributor, comma, distribution date, close bracket, full stop.

Example footnote for a film:

[1]*1001 Pranks*, dir. by Joe Kerr (English Film Enterprises, 2015).

WHAT IF IT'S A TELEVISION EPISODE?

For an individual episode on television, write the title of the episode in single quotation marks, followed by a comma. Then write the name of the series in italics and then a full stop. Write the series number, a comma, the episode number and a full stop. Finally, write the television channel, a comma, the date the episode was aired, another comma and, if available, the time of transmission. End with a full stop.

Example footnote for an episode from a television series:

[1]'It's only Monday', *A Week in the Day of an English Teacher*. Series 1, episode 2. TW2, 13 March 2015, 9.30pm.

WHAT IF IT'S A TELEVISION PROGRAMME?

Write the name of the series it italics. Then write the television channel, the date the episode was aired and, if available, the time of transmission. Separate the information with commas and end with a full stop.

Example footnote for a television programme:

[1]*Les Plack the Dentist*, TW2, 13 March 2015, 9.30pm.

WHAT IF I'VE WATCHED THE TELEVISION SERIES OR PROGRAMME ON THE INTERNET?

If you've downloaded a programme to watch on BBC iPlayer, for example, follow the time of transmission, you add the date that you accessed your episode or programme in square brackets.

Example footnote for an episode from a television series that you have viewed on the internet:

[1]'Icebergs', *Global Warming*. Series 1, episode 2. TW2 [Accessed 31 March 2015].

Example footnote for a general television programme viewed on the internet:

[1]*The Indifference of Luke Warm*, TW2 [accessed 31 March 2015].

WHAT IF I'VE WATCHED A FILM IN A CINEMA?

As a minimum, you need to include the title, director, distributor and date of distribution.

Example footnote for a film:

[1]*Making Waves*, dir. by C. Shore (21st Century Seascape, 2015).

WHAT IF I'VE WATCHED A TELEVISION EPISODE, PROGRAMME OR FILM ON A DVD?

For a television episode or programme, include the same information as you would to record them from the internet, but replace the access date with 'DVD':

Example footnote for an episode from a television series that you have viewed on a DVD:

[1]'Max Little', *Identity Crisis*. Series 1, episode 2. TW2 [DVD].

Example footnote for a general television programme viewed on a DVD:

[1]*Identity Crisis*, TW2 [DVD].

If you have watched a film on a DVD, record the same information as you did in the film footnote example, but at the end add '[DVD]':

Example footnote for a film:

[1]*Who took the Microphone?* Dir. by Mike Stand (21st Century Baboon, 2015) [DVD].

WHAT IF IT'S A BLOG POST?

Record the writer's name, the title of the blog in quotation marks, the full URL and the date accessed.

Example footnote for a blog:

[1]Carol Singer, 'The Tunes of Christmas', http://www.carolsblog/blog [accessed 31 March 2015].

WHAT IF IT'S A TWITTER POST?

First, you need to hunt down the original tweet rather than quoting a retweet. In your footnote, introduce it as a tweet and state the writer's real name. Quote the tweet, keeping any #hashtags. Use the same spelling and punctuation as the original post. Finally, record the writer's @handle/user name and the date of the tweet in brackets. For example:

Example footnote for a tweet:

[1]Kerry Lewis tweets in order to spread her love of spelling, punctuation and grammar: '#SPaG is for life—not just the classroom'. (@Mrs_SPaG, 31 March 2015).

WHAT IF IT'S A FACEBOOK POST?

At the time of writing (spring 2015), Facebook has become less popular with your age group; however, if you do cite a Facebook post, follow the same formula as for a tweet.

Multiple Citations

You might be wondering if you have to repeat all of the above information if you cite the same text a second time. The short answer is no.

HOW DO IF I CITE THE SAME REFERENCE IF IT APPEARS AT LEAST TWICE IN A ROW?

If you use the same reference at least twice in a row and your second reference is immediately after your first, write the word **ibid**, which means 'in the same source'. Then write your new page number. See example overleaf.

Citing from the same text at least twice in a row:

[1] Earl Lee Riser, *A New Age Dawns*, 2nd edn (New York: Sunrise Publications, 2014), pp. 83-96.

[2]Ibid., p. 101.

[3]Ibid., p. 72.

WHAT IF I CITE THE SAME SOURCE, BUT IT'S LATER IN THE ESSAY?

If you mention the same source in your essay, but there are other footnotes referring to other sources in between, write the author's surname and the page number(s). For example:

Citing from the same source later in an essay:

¹Earl Lee Riser, *A New Age Dawns*, 2nd edn (New York: Sunrise Publications, 2014), pp. 83-96.

²Sally Forth, *Travels of a Lady*, (London: Travel Tips, 2015), pp. 106-10.

³Riser, p. 214.

WHAT IF I REFERENCE AN AUTHOR, WHO HAS WRITTEN DIFFERENT BOOKS?

If you have used two or more books from the same author in your essay, add a shortened title in order to avoid confusion. For example:

Citing from the same author but different texts:

¹Earl Lee Riser, *A New Age Dawns*, 2nd edn (New York: Sunrise Publications, 2014), pp. 83-96.

²Earl Lee Riser, *End of an Era*, (New York: Sunrise Publications, 2015), pp. 106-10.

³Riser, *New Age*, p. 214.

WHAT IF I REFERENCE THE BIBLE?

When you quote from the Bible, you do not create a footnote. Instead, put the references in brackets in your essay. You must insert a colon between chapter and verse, and always use Arabic (not Roman) numerals.

Citing the Bible:

However, clay can be shaped into new forms; in the Bible, when God created Adam, he 'formed the man of dust from the ground' (Gen. 2:8).

The chart below summarises the biblical text abbreviations. You must use these when your references are in brackets.

Genesis	**Gen.**	**Nahum**	**Nah.**
Exodus	Ex.	Habbakuk	Hab.
Leviticus	Lev.	Zephaniah	Zeph.
Numbers	Num.	Haggai	Hag.
Deuteronomy	Deut. *or* Dt.	Zechariah	Zech.
Joshua	Josh.	Malachi	Mal.
Judges	Jdg.	Matthew	Matt.
Ruth	Ruth	Mark	Mk.
1 Samuel	1 Sam.	Luke	Lk.
2 Samuel	2 Sam.	John	Jn.

1 Kings	1 Kgs.	Acts	Acts *or* Ac.
2 Kings	2 Kgs.	Romans	Rom.
1 Chronicles	1 Chron. *or* 1 Chr.	1 Corinthians	1 Cor.
2 Chronicles	2 Chron. *or* 2 Chr.	2 Corinthians	2 Cor.
Ezra	Ezra	Galatians	Gal.
Nehemiah	Neh.	Ephesians	Eph.
Esther	Est.	Phillipians	Phil.
Job	Job	1 Thessalonians	1 Thess.
Psalms	Ps.	2 Thessalonians	2 Thess.
Proverbs	Prov.	1 Timothy	1 Tim.
Ecclesiastes	Ecc.	2 Timothy	2 Tim.
Song of Songs	Song.	Titus	Tit.
Isaiah	Is.	Philemon	Phile. *or* Philem.
Jeremiah	Jer.	Hebrews	Heb.
Lamentations	Lam.	James	Jas.
Ezekiel	Ezek. or Ez.	1 Peter	1 Pet.

Daniel	Dan.	2 Peter	2 Pet.
Hosea	Hos.	1 John	1 Jn.
Joel	Joel	2 John	2 Jn.
Amos	Am.	3 John	3 Jn.
Obadiah	Obad.	Jude	Jude
Jonah	Jon.	Revelation	Rev.
Micah	Mic.	Colossians	Col.

If you refer to a whole text from the Bible in your sentence, you must write its name in full:

Citing a Biblical text in your sentence:

In **Genesis**, the creationist theory is introduced. We learn that when God created Adam, he 'formed the man of dust from the ground' (Gen. 2:8).

Bibliography

You now know how to write footnotes and there is one final task: the bibliography, which summarises all of your wider reading. **Only include the texts that you have referred to in your essay. Remember to include your primary sources** as well as your secondary sources!

Generally speaking, a longer a bibliography demonstrates wider reading and more informed ideas. A good bibliography shows your teacher and the moderator that you have conducted an impressive amount of research.

Finally, the exam boards require you to keep a hard copy of all internet materials used; they recommend that your teacher collects these so that they can be used for reference purposes if necessary.

HOW DO I WRITE A BIBLIOGRAPHY?

1. List all of your primary and secondary sources in alphabetical order by the author's or editor's surname, followed by the forename or initial.
2. If you have more than one author or editor, write the first surname and forename or initial. Keep the remaining names as forename or initial followed by surname.
3. Delete all page numbers except page ranges for book chapters and journals.
4. Do not put a full stop at the end of each source

EXAMPLE BIBLIOGRAPHY

This example bibliography overleaf is based on the texts used in the footnote examples, above. I have also included two fictitious primary sources.

Bibliography

Bruff, Mr., *Grammar Tuesday: A* Rhetorical Devices,* online video recording, YouTube, 3 February 2015 https://youtu.be/i5Mxud7yP9Y?list=PLqGFsWf-P-cAs4w- AQ9_5izpACHpxM0HN [accessed March 31, 2015]

Bull, Terry, *The Trials and Tribulations of Life*, 3rd edn (London: Hangman Books, 2013)

Case, Charity, 'The Plight of the Poor', *Philanthropic Journal,* 46 (2015), 58-68

Forth, Sally, *Travels of a Lady*, (London: Travel Tips, 2015)

'Icebergs', *Global Warming*. Series 1, episode 2. TW2 [Accessed 31 March 2015]

Identity Crisis, TW2 [DVD]

'It's only Monday', *A Week in the Day of an English Teacher*. Series 1, episode 2. TW2, 13 March 2015, 9.30pm

Jellow, O., 'Colours', in *The Rainbow,* ed. by Paige Turner (Paris: Eiffel Books, 2015), pp. 178-263

Kerr, Joe, dir., *1001 Pranks*, dir. (English Film Enterprises, 2015)

Kinn, Manny, *Pins, Needles and Fabrics: My Story*, (London: Stitch Publications, 2013)

Liver, D., *Happy Households* (London: Project Post, 2008), https://www.post.org/files/1342-h.htm [accessed 31 March 2015]

Les Plack the Dentist, TW2, 13 March 2015, 9.30pm

Lewis, Kerry, *Mr Bruff's Guide to Grammar,* ed. by A. Bruff (2014, MrBruffEnglish), Kindle edition

Lewis, Kerry, Twitter (@Mrs_SPaG, 31 March 2015)

Lowe, B., 'Underground Caverns', *Twiddleswick News,* 1 April 2015

'Max Little', *Identity Crisis*. Series 1, episode 2. TW2 [DVD]

Major, D. and A. Minor, *Literary Notes* (London: Chime Publications, 2015)

Riser, Earl Lee, *A New Age Dawns*, 2nd edn (New York: Sunrise Publications, 2014)

Riser, Earl, Lee, *End of an Era*, (New York: Sunrise Publications, 2015)

Shore, C., dir. *Making Waves*, (21st Century Seascape, 2015)

Singer, Carol, 'The Tunes of Christmas', http://www.carolsblog/blog/ [accessed 31 March 2015]

Spag, K., 'The Beauty of Grammar', *British Grammar Journal,* 46 (2015), http://www.britishgrammarjournal.co.uk [accessed 31 March 2015]

Stand, Mike, dir., *Who took the Microphone?* (21st Century Baboon, 2015) [DVD]

Morris, Hugh, 'Laugh at Life', *Twiddleswick News,* 1 April 2015, in 'twiddleswick.co.uk', http://www.twiddleswick.co.uk/news/laugh/life, [accessed 31 March 2015]

Storm, Gail, 'Why the Tempest Calls', *Twiddleswick News,* 1 April 2015, Twiddleswick travel supplement

The Indifference of Luke Warm, TW2 [accessed 31 March 2015]

Three Critical Approaches, (London: Triclops, n.d.),
   http://www.triclops.com/three/critical/approaches/ [accessed March 31, 2015]

Do I need to have Footnotes and a Bibliography my Exams?

The short and I am sure most welcome answer is no. You only need to acknowledge your wider reading through footnotes and a bibliography with the non-exam assessment, which your teacher marks. This is because you will have had more time to think about your non-examined texts and to research them independently.

In the exams, you would be expected to quote or refer to your wider reading.

IMPORTANT NOTE

From this point onwards, references and footnotes will be used in example writing so that you can familiarise yourself with these techniques.

Sometimes, I have been unable to quote directly from my sources for copyright reasons, so I have summarised my reading instead. **In your non-exam assessment, you would be expected to quote.**

So Which Parts of AO1 are assessed in my Exams?

When the examiner is assessing you against AO1 criteria in the exam, he or she will be looking for:

- An excellent understanding of text

- Consistently fluent and accurate writing

- Accurate use of concepts/terminology

- A well-structured and coherent argument

In the next chapter, we will begin to examine AO2, which assesses how meanings are shaped.

Chapter 7

AO2: How Meanings are Shaped

Assessment Objective 2 requires you to:

> **Analyse ways in which meanings are shaped in literary texts.**

The additional ways in which meanings can be shaped will be discussed at the end of this chapter.

In a nutshell, AO2 assesses your ability to explore and explain a text: these skills are called **analytical methods**.

Analytical Methods

You are now experts on form, structure and language; however, as we saw in earlier chapters, knowing the terminology isn't enough. You might, for example, choose to show how a poet takes an image and treats it in a variety of ways during a poem, or show how a novelist structures a chapter.

In this guide, there are lots of examples of analytical methods being demonstrated, including one at the end of this chapter.

Another **analytical method** is your ability to quote. Your quotations must be appropriate to the question and be used thoughtfully to support the direction of your argument.

HOW TO QUOTE

As you are studying for an A' level in English Literature, you will probably have gained at least a grade C in your GCSE English literature. This means that you should already have the skill to select quotations and embed them into your sentences. This section will therefore briefly revise how to quote.

Firstly, a reminder that when you are quoting the exact words of a text, you need single quotation marks to distinguish the other person's words from yours. Do not use double inverted commas because these are speech marks, not quotation marks.

If you are quoting short words and phrases or up to two full lines of a poem, you need to embed them into your sentences.

Example Embedded Quotation:

When Abraham Lincoln said that a person 'cannot escape the responsibility of tomorrow by evading it today', he meant that he did not want to avoid difficult tasks such as abolishing slavery and uniting America.

If the quotation is longer, separate it from the main text and indent it. Omit the quotation marks.

Example Separated Quotation:

One of the most famous openings in literature is in Jane Austen's *Pride and Prejudice:*

It is a truth universally acknowledged that a single man in possession of a good fortune must be in want of a wife.

However little known the feelings or views of such a man may be on his first entering a neighbourhood, this truth is so well fixed in the minds of the surrounding families, that he is considered the rightful property of someone or other of their daughters.

PUNCTUATION WITH QUOTATIONS

Full Stop

First of all, a reminder that the full stop goes at the end of your sentence, after the quotation mark. If the quotation ends in a full stop in the original text, leave it out: *your* full stop is more important.

Example Punctuation:

Mr Darcy 'had ten thousand a year'.

Ellipsis (...)

You might sometimes want to omit non-essential words from a quotation. For example, the following sentence is rather long:

Before Ellipsis:

Mr. Darcy soon drew the attention of the room by his fine, tall person, handsome features, noble mien, and the report which was in general circulation within five minutes after his entrance, of his having ten thousand a year.

I am now going to embed the above quotation into my sentence and omit some of the words, replacing them with ellipsis (...):

With Ellipsis:

When Mr. Darcy arrived at the ball, he attracted 'attention' because of 'his fine, tall person, handsome features, noble mien, and the report...of his having ten thousand a year'.

If you're not sure if your sentence with embedded quotations is grammatically correct, imagine deleting the quotation marks. Your sentence should make perfect grammatical sense. For example:

Grammar test:

When Mr. Darcy arrived at the ball, he attracted attention because of his fine, tall person, handsome features, noble mien, and the report...of his having ten thousand a year.

Square Brackets [ ]

If you add your own words to a quotation, put them in square brackets to show that they are not part of the original text.

Example use of Square Brackets:

When Mr. Darcy arrived at the ball, he attracted the 'attention of the room [in other words, the people] by his fine, tall person, handsome features, noble mien, and the report ... of his having ten thousand a year'.

Double Quotation Marks " "

Use double quotation marks for a quotation within a quotation. For example:

Example of Quotation within a Quotation:

The minister said 'To say the NHS is "robust" is a blatant lie'.

Colon

A colon introduces a quotation that's roughly a sentence long:

Example of a Colon to Introduce a Quotation:

In *Pride and Prejudice* Mr Bingley is Mr Darcy's foil: 'Bingley was sure of being liked wherever he appeared, Darcy was continually giving offence'.

Aim to embed short quotations into your sentences where you can, as this is a higher level skill.

INTRODUCING QUOTATIONS

Never, ever, ever quote a sentence without introducing it first. Even worse, never, ever, ever have a sentence that is just a quotation and nothing else.

Instead, consider introducing your quotation with some of these verbs. *The writer...*

> argues, asserts, challenges, claims, comments, concludes, considers, contrasts, counters, defends, demonstrates, depicts, establishes, explains, explores, exposes, illustrates, imagines, indicates, insists, introduces, investigates, maintains, notes, observes, outlines, points out, presents, questions, says, reveals, states, suggests, summarises, writes...

This is not an exhaustive list, but it is a useful starting point. Here are some more phrases:

> According to X, ...
>
> As X has noted, ...
>
> In the words of X, ...
>
> In X's view, ...
>
> X says that...

X states that...

Whichever 'signal' verb or phrase you choose, check that you understand its nuances so that you use it correctly.

How Meanings are Shaped

Exam boards encourage you to broaden your analytical skills by moving beyond analysing structure, form and language. This is why the wording of the assessment objective encourages you to analyse *the ways* in which meanings are shaped.

You can still analyse structure, form and language, but you should also weave in your knowledge of context, consider literary theory and the views of others where appropriate. These all influence how meanings are shaped, and you are demonstrating how this knowledge informs your ideas.

However, don't allow them to dominate: your opinion is more important.

At GCSE, you may have learnt to develop an analysis by using the PEE (point, evidence, explanation) or PEA (point, evidence, analysis) paragraphing models. This is excellent for building your ideas, but the disadvantage is that each paragraph tends to focus on one specific quotation. Consequently, you might struggle to develop your ideas and you might even repeat the same point in different words.

At A' level, you're expected to pick apart quotations, explore layers of meaning and cross-reference your ideas with other parts of the text. This adds more weight to your views and demonstrates a **detailed critical understanding**.

As your focus is on the key words of the question, a blended approach in which you integrate your knowledge of the elements that we have studied so far is more effective.

Example of How Meanings are Shaped

On the next page is an example analysis that focuses on the character of Shylock in Shakespeare's *The Merchant of Venice*. In order to understand the references, first read two extracts from the play.

In the first, Solanio, an unsympathetic Christian, is telling his friend about the Jewish moneylender Shylock, whose daughter, Jessica, has eloped with a Christian called Lorenzo. Jessica has also stolen Shylock's money (ducats) and valuables:

I never heard a passion so confused,

So strange, outrageous, and so variable,

As the dog Jew did utter in the streets.

"My daughter! O my ducats! O my daughter,

Fled with a Christian! O my Christian ducats!

Justice, the law, my ducats, and my daughter!

A sealèd bag, two sealèd bags of ducats,

Of double ducats, stol'n from me by my daughter!

And jewels—two stones, two rich and precious stones—

Stol'n by my daughter! Justice, find the girl!

She hath the stones upon her, and the ducats."

—Act 2, Scene 8

In the next Act, Shylock explains the ways in which he is the same as a Christian.

Hath not a Jew eyes? hath not a Jew hands, organs, dimensions, senses, affections, passions? Fed with the same food, hurt with the same weapons, subject to the same diseases, healed by the same means, warmed and cooled by the same winter and summer, as a Christian is? If you prick us, do we not bleed? If you tickle us, do we not laugh? If you poison us, do we not die? And if you wrong us, shall we not revenge? If we are like you in the rest, we will resemble you in that. If a Jew wrong a Christian, what is his humility? Revenge. If a Christian wrong a Jew, what should his sufferance be by Christian example? Why, revenge. The villainy you teach me, I will execute, and it shall go hard but I will better the instruction.

—Act 3, Scene 1

Now read these extracts the example analysis, below. Pay particular attention to the phrases in **bold** because they link to how meanings are shaped.

Example Analysis: How Meanings are Shaped

Shylock, the **antagonist** of *The Merchant of Venice* is both a villain and a victim of circumstances beyond his control. His **character** is needed to drive the **'pound of flesh'** revenge element of the **plot** forward; he is also a **device** to impede the love of three young couples, including in the **sub-plot** that of his daughter, Jessica, who elopes with Lorenzo. He therefore functions as an important **catalyst** to events in the play.

When Jessica elopes, Solanio pitilessly reports Shylock's reaction, turning him into an object of fun. According to Solanio (and we only have Solanio's interpretation of events), Shylock values his daughter as much as his money **("My daughter! O my ducats! O my daughter...O my Christian ducats!"). The contemporary audience is expected to laugh with** Solanio, owing to prevalent racist attitudes towards Jews.[1]

The actor playing Solanio might have encouraged this further by imitating Shylock's voice and exaggerating his gestures. Moreover, Solanio speaks in **blank verse**, which lends authority to his words and, in a sense, gives the audience permission to follow his example and laugh at Shylock. Moreover, when Solanio quotes Shylock, it is clear from the breakdown of **iambic pentameter** that the moneylender was originally speaking in **prose**, which was used by low-status characters, particularly **comic figures**.[2] This therefore supports the idea that Shylock is an object of ridicule.

However, there is depth to Shylock's character elsewhere in the play, and a **modern audience** in particular might sympathise with him in the aspects of his life that drive him to behave in the way that he does. In his famous **'I am a Jew. Hath not a Jew eyes?'** speech, Shylock employs an impressive range of **rhetorical devices** to **emphasise the prejudices of society**. These devices include seven **rhetorical questions, lists of passive verbs + preposition + definite article + repetition of adjective + noun ('fed with the same food, hurt with the same weapons, subject to the same diseases')** and the **repetition** of a **rhetorical question** with the answer 'revenge' ('If a Jew wrong a Christian, what is his humility? Revenge'). **Although the speech is written in prose, there is nothing comic about it**. The prose emphasises Shylock's heartfelt eloquence and, by the end of the **speech, the audience feels** a mixture of empathy for Shylock as well as horror that he will 'better the instruction' of his enemies. It is therefore difficult to believe that he is a **stereotypical** evil **villain**, as Shakespeare continually manipulates the audience's feelings about him to create a complex character.

COMMENTARY

The phrases in **red** demonstrate an awareness of the **analytical methods** being used to evaluate the character of Shylock. As well as picking apart structure, form and language, the reactions of the contemporary audience have been woven into the analysis and contrasted with those of a modern audience.

This analysis could have been expanded, however. For example, the character of Shylock might have been compared to depictions of other Jews in contemporary literature. He might also have been compared to depictions of other minority characters in Shakespearean plays.

Other people's interpretations have not been included or considered.

The wider your reading, the more detail you will be able to include, thereby demonstrating a **detailed understanding** of how meanings are shaped.

This leads neatly to the next assessment objective, which assesses your knowledge of context. Let's explore this further.

Chapter 8

AO3: What is Context?

AO3 requires you to:

Demonstrate understanding of the significance and influence of the contexts in which literary texts are written and received.

Some people define context as a backdrop; in other words, what was happening when the text was set. Another definition is anything beyond the words of the text that help you to understand its meaning. There are different kinds of context and they often overlap. Some examples are below, and you might encounter more in your own reading.

It's always useful to know about context because your awareness of events will improve your understanding and analysis of character, theme and authorial intention.

Biographical Context

This is information about the author's life, which might help you to understand his or her choice of subject matter and attitudes within the text.

For example, Charles Dickens hated trains. Trains were a marvellous Victorian invention, so why were his views so negative? On 9th June, 1865, he was in the Staplehurst rail crash in which his train was derailed, killing ten passengers and injuring forty. The accident affected him so badly that he lost his voice for two weeks and for the rest of his life, he avoided travelling by train if he could.

In his short story *The Signal-Man*, he describes a railway cutting with its 'dripping-wet wall[s] of jagged stone' as a 'great dungeon' with a 'gloomy red light' at the entrance of a 'black tunnel', which has a 'barbarous, depressing, and forbidding air.' There is 'an earthy deadly smell' and 'cold wind rushed through it'. His fear and trepidation of railways can clearly be seen in his use of death imagery and the sense of being trapped.

Cultural Context

The cultural context refers to the beliefs, values, ideas, customs and behaviour that people have at the time a text is written or set. These ideas might be influenced by a person's gender, race, age or class, or by their attitudes to others of a different gender, race, age or class. The cultural context relates to attitudes that are considered normal in a particular society.

Published in 1852, *Uncle Tom's Cabin* by Harriet Beecher Stowe was the second-best selling book of the nineteenth century after the Bible. A year after it was published, 300,000 copies had been sold in America; this was an incredibly high number for the time. The abolitionist movement was stronger in the UK where over a million copies were sold.

At that time, slavery in America was legal and—in the Deep South—acceptable. Stowe shows her readers the reality of slavery in an attempt to challenge contemporary attitudes and develop a new anti-slavery culture.

Geographical Context

Considering the geographical context or settings can help to deepen your understanding of texts.

In Jane Austen's *Pride and Prejudice*, for example, Lydia leaves her family for a holiday in Brighton, which is on the south coast. Because of the conduct of the Prince Regent, who spent a lot of his leisure time there, the seaside town had a reputation for loose behaviour. This location therefore symbolises danger for the badly-chaperoned Lydia.

When she and Mr Wickham disappear in London, the setting is appropriate for their illicit relationship, as London is an easy place in which to hide. Lydia eventually marries Mr Wickham and they move to the north of England, symbolising that they will never as a couple be welcome at the heart of respectable society.

In contrast, when Lydia's sister Elizabeth travels, she visits Derbyshire, which is in the centre of England and as far away from the coast as it is possible to get—not only this, but she is chaperoned by her aunt and uncle. This represents her status as a respectable young lady in a polite, safe environment; moreover, Derbyshire was known as a fashionable beauty spot and so it was a socially acceptable place to visit.

With the Peak District being a beauty spot, this adds an air of romance to her holiday.

In literature, there might be real geographical settings, fictional places located in actual settings, or imaginary places. Always consider which geographical features are real and why they have been included; whether these features are essential to the story; whether the geography limits the story; and the extent to which the writer has altered geography as well as possible reasons for this.

Historical Context

Quite often, this has links to other kinds of contexts such as cultural, political, social, personal and literary. Consider key historical events that influence the writer's purpose. For example, when studying World War I poetry, you cannot ignore the war, its impact on the soldiers, on non-combatants, and on later generations. Attitudes at the beginning of the war were also different to those at the end; writers such as Wilfred Owen and Siegfried Sassoon chose to describe the harsh reality of war, which was a direct contrast to the earlier patriotic sonnets of Rupert Brook. If Brook hadn't died in 1915, it would have been interesting to see if his poetry had evolved along the same lines as Owen and Sassoon.

Texts might also be set in or deliberately reference an earlier historical period. H.G. Wells in his horror story *The Red Room* makes a point of describing unfriendly 'old people' an 'old mirror' and other 'old-fashioned furniture' to develop the idea of 'another age, an older age, an age when things spiritual were indeed to be feared, when common sense was uncommon, an age when omens and witches were credible, and ghosts beyond denying'. This plants seeds in the reader's mind, suggesting that supernatural events are possible, making later events more terrifying.

Literary Context

It's always interesting to investigate texts that are referenced within the poems, plays or novels that you are studying. In *Northanger Abbey*, Jane Austen says: 'Milton, Pope, and Prior, with a paper from the Spectator, and a chapter from Sterne, are eulogized by a thousand pens'. This reflects contemporary attitudes to literature, which was expected to improve the mind.

References to contemporary literature can also tell you a lot about the characters. In *Northanger Abbey*, Isabella lends her new friend, the naïve Catherine, a sensational Gothic romance *The Mysteries of Udolpho* by Ann Radcliffe. Isabella also waxes lyrical about *Castle of Wolfenbach, Clermont, Mysterious Warnings, Necromancer of the Black Forest, Midnight Bell, Orphan of the Rhine,* and *Horrid Mysteries.* By the titles, it is quite clear that they are not novels that were written to improve the mind, as they fall into the Gothic genre that was so popular at the time. Austen therefore— through Isabella's choice of reading matter—hints that she is not a desirable friend for our heroine Catherine.

At the time, novels were frowned upon, and Austen wryly comments on contemporary attitudes, 'undervaluing the labour of the novelist and of slighting the performances which have only genius, wit, and taste to recommend them'. It's amusing to note that reading novels, generally considered an inferior type of literature, was a form of teenage rebellion.

You might also want to read other texts by the same author, looking for similarities and differences in characterisation, themes, language, form and structure.

Finally, it's always interesting to read texts that share a theme, are part of a literary movement (see chapter 9) or the same genre (see chapter 10).

Political Context

This links to the political background of a text and sometimes the author's political views, which might be linked to the social context.

In order to appreciate Victor Hugo's *Les Miserables*, it helps to understand the political and social context of the French Revolution, which began with the storming of the Bastille in 1789. It is then easier to appreciate Hugo's vision of nineteenth century French politics as, forty-three years after the revolution began, his main characters symbolise larger problems within nineteenth century French society. *Les Miserables* is therefore about the *legacy* of the French Revolution.

Politics might also influence decisions about what to include or omit in a text. Shakespeare wrote *Macbeth*, knowing full well that the reigning monarch King James I of England (also King James VI of Scotland) was interested in witches. The King, who had written a book about witches and was responsible for the persecution, arrest, torture and execution of many innocent women, was also the patron of

Shakespeare's acting company. It made sense therefore for Shakespeare to include witches in the opening scene of the play to attract royal interest.

Not only that, but King James I was known to be descended from Banquo; this fulfils the witches' prophecy in the play that his descendants would rule. It would have pleased the King to watch confirmation in the play of his divine right to rule.

Religious or Philosophical Context

An awareness of the religious of philosophical context will help you to understand people's ways of thinking.

For example, in John Webster's *The Duchess of Malfi*, (first performed around 1613) there is a corrupt, murderous Cardinal of the Roman Catholic Church. His character is so evil that in 1618, Orazio Busino, the chaplain to the Venetian ambassador to England, complained about how Catholics—particularly the character of the Cardinal—were depicted. It is unlikely that the Protestant audience had much sympathy for Busino's views: some would have had lived through Queen Mary's persecution of Protestants (1554-58); others will have been familiar with John Foxe's *The Book of Martyrs* (published 1563), which describes the religious persecution of Protestants by Catholics. It would also have been common knowledge that Queen Elizabeth I was excommunicated from the Catholic Church in 1570 and that the Catholic Mary Queen of Scots (executed for treason in 1587) had unsuccessfully plotted to overthrow her. The idea that God was on the side of the Protestants would have been confirmed in 1588 when England defeated the Catholic Spanish Armada.

Social and Economic Contexts

As stated above, the social and economic contexts are often connected. The legal context might also be important.

For example, when the New Poor Law was introduced in 1834, it had a huge impact on the destitute. From this year onwards, they had to go to workhouses where families were split up, given workhouse clothes and poor quality food. They were forced to toil for long hours to pay for their keep. The philosophy behind this was that unemployed poor people were in that position because they were too lazy to look for work. The workhouse therefore served as a deterrent: the poor would regard the conditions as so appalling that they would rather look for work.

Charles Dickens strongly disagreed with this philosophy, as he knew that unemployed people were not necessarily lazy. At the age of twelve, his father had been imprisoned for debt, so Dickens had had no choice but to leave school and work. Having lived through poverty, he was sympathetic towards the plight of the poor. In his novel *Oliver Twist,* he uses sarcasm to ridicule the 'very sage, deep, philosophical men' on the poor law boards: 'they established the rule, that all poor people should have the alternative...of being starved by a gradual process in the [work] house, or by a quick one out of it'. As a result of his early experience, many of his novels, such as *A Christmas Carol* and *Hard Times*, are social commentaries, dealing with the theme of poverty.

Theatrical Context

The theatrical context can reveal a lot about the attitudes of a contemporary audience. Consider the date that a play was first performed and the nature of the theatre-goers. Did people from a range of social classes go to the theatre, or were plays aimed at the elite? What were the norms of social behaviour at the time and to what extent did playwrights conform to or challenge these norms? For example, Richard Sheridan's *The Rivals* (1775) was written at a time when people followed elaborate codes of learned socially acceptable behaviour. Consequently, the characters in Sheridan's play are constrained by the rules of politeness and good breeding. Sheridan satirizes this concept through some of his characters challenging the notion of conforming: instead, they display elements of modern individualism. Consider too the reactions of a contemporary audience and contrast it with those of a modern audience.

How do I use my Knowledge of Context?

Tailor your knowledge to the question: wider reading is fantastic, but there's no point in writing everything you know, regardless of its relevance.

Equally, there's no point in tagging your knowledge of an important contextual point at the end of a paragraph because then you won't have explored it.

Aim to weave your knowledge into the point that you are making. This way, you are showing the reader how your awareness of context is informing your point of view.

EXAMPLE

Read the example below.

Example of weaving context into writing:

Uncle Tom's Cabin by Harriet Beecher Stowe, published in 1852 and set in America when slavery was legal, was the second-best selling book of the nineteenth century after the Bible.[1] **This fact alone reflects** the anti-slavery sentiment, not just within America but also the United Kingdom. There is also a story that when the president Abraham Lincoln met Stowe at the start of the Civil War, he said, 'So this is the little lady who started this great war.'[2] **Whether this story is to be believed is open to question;** it was recounted by Stowe's son, who would have been biased and might have exaggerated his mother's reputation. **Nevertheless, the anecdote raises an interesting point about** the power of literature to effect social change at a time when abolitionists were—like Stowe—condemning slavery as un-Christian. **Laudable as its aims were, the impact of *Uncle Tom's Cabin* in a modern cultural context is weaker**, as many of Stove's characters have been interpreted as racial stereotypes; for example, the long-suffering, faithful servant and the 'pickaninny' children. **Nevertheless, its impact as a contemporary anti-slavery novel cannot be underestimated**, and many believe that it helped to lay the groundwork of the American Civil War.

---

[1]Gail K. Smith, 'The Sentimental Novel: The Example of Harriet Beecher Stowe', in *The Cambridge Companion to Nineteenth-Century American Women's Writing* ed. by Dale M. Bauer and Philip Gould (London: Cambridge University Press, 2001), p. 221.

[2]Charles Edward Stowe, *Harriet Beecher Stowe: The Story of Her Life* (Boston: Houghton Mifflin Company, 1911) p. 203.

COMMENTARY

From the example analysis, it is clear that the writer is not simply explaining her knowledge of context. The phrases in **red** introduce analytical commentary, which illustrates how the writer's knowledge of context informs her understanding and interpretation of the novel.

To Conclude

There are other elements of context; one of these is to consider the literary movement that was taking place at the time your text was written. We will explore this in the next chapter.

Chapter 9

AO3: Literary Periods and Movements

A literary period or movement is a writing trend over a particular period of time in which novelists, playwrights and poets have similar approaches to their work. They often write about similar themes and sometimes employ the same genre.

At the time that they were alive, poets, novelists and dramatists will not have been aware that they were part of a named literary movement. This came much later when academics analysed and categorised similarities between groups of writers and their works.

To demonstrate your knowledge of context, you might identify the literary movement into which your text falls and examine the extent to which the text fits into the respective movement.

Below is an introduction to some literary periods in Britain and other literary periods that overlapped them, either in Britain or abroad. Use these overviews as a starting point for your wider reading.

It is important to be aware that time frames are sometimes blurred, so some authors do not always fit comfortably within a particular literary period. Jane Austen, for example, falls into the Romantic Movement, but stylistically her work more closely resembles that of the earlier neo-classical period. Likewise, Charlotte and Emily Bronte wrote their novels in the Victorian era, but their writing contains the themes and stylistic features of the Romantic period.

Some example writers from each literary movement are included in the summaries below. You are likely to encounter many more in the course of your wider reading.

Main Literary Movements in Britain

MEDIEVAL: 500-1500

This period covers an impressive thousand years of literature in which early medieval tails were transcribed onto manuscripts from oral storytelling. A famous example is *Beowulf* (1,000), which was written in Anglo-Saxon.

People also wrote in Latin, French, Welsh, Old English and different Middle English dialects. Author and scholar The Venerable Bede, also known as The Father of

English History wrote in Latin. His most famous work (c. 731) translates as *The Ecclesiastical History of the English People*. More than 600 years later, Geoffrey Chaucer's *The Canterbury Tales* (c. 1390) was written in Middle English.

The Catholic Church held the power in medieval times so religious texts were the most popular. Common themes included revenge and forgiveness; allegories were also popular, with characters personified as Charity, Faith, etc. Romances were the second most popular, and the stories of King Arthur sprang from this period.

With the arrival of the printing press in 1473, books could be mass produced for the first time, heralding the advent of the next literary movement.

ENGLISH RENAISSANCE: (OR EARLY MODERN PERIOD) 1485-1700

There is a lot of debate about when the English renaissance begins: some scholars date it from 1500 while others mark it as beginning in 1485 when Henry Tudor won the Battle of Bosworth.

The word *renaissance* means rebirth of learning. It holds the idea of moving out of the Dark Ages, with its memories of the Black Death, into exciting and optimistic times.

Ancient Greek and Roman texts influenced the renaissance writer and these texts were, in a sense, reborn in new writings. People studied grammar, rhetoric, history, poetry and moral philosophy—look for evidence of them in the crafting of your renaissance writer's work.

With the arrival of the printing press, more texts began to be mass produced in English. A culture of poetry and drama emerged with Shakespeare, Francis Bacon, John Donne, Ben Johnson, Edmund Spenser, Christopher Marlowe and Thomas Wyatt. These renaissance poets and dramatists tended to focus on human existence, particularly the themes of human potential and love.

ENLIGHTENMENT (OR THE AGE OF REASON): 1650s-1780s

Towards the end of the English renaissance, Francis Bacon composed philosophical treatises, which dealt with facts, evidence and conclusions. These treatises inspired modern scientific methods. Another important text was Isaac Newton's *Principia* (1687), which became the foundation of physics.

This was therefore a time of advances in science and rationalism. Not afraid to express their views, intellectuals debated and argued, with many rejecting organised religion, instead favouring a more personal way of worshipping. The poet Alexander Pope captured the mood of the times when he wrote: 'Know then thyself; presume not God to scan. /The proper study of mankind is man.' The study of humans became far more interesting than the study of God.

Augustan literature flourished in the first half of the 18th century. Augustan poetry was named after Caesar Augustus, Emperor of Rome (63 BC-14 AD). The **English Augustans** translated Roman poets from that time (Ovid, Virgil, Propertius and Horace among others) and imitated their writing style.

Being clever and witty was now the fashion; parody and satire became a popular method of poking fun at institutions. A famous novel from this movement is Jonathan Swift's *Gulliver's Travels*, which satirises human nature and parodies travellers' tales. Alexander Pope also savagely criticised eighteenth century English society in *The Dunciad* ('a wit with dunces and a dunce with wits'). The fashion of Augustan literature ended in the 1740s when Pope and Swift died.

Although poetry remained popular, much of the new **neoclassical** literature (Western literature that is inspired by classical literature from Ancient Rome and Ancient Greece) was nonfiction: it aimed, with its emphasis on facts, to be realistic. If it made people think, instructed and enlightened them, it was considered to be good literature. It was formal, well-ordered, well-structured writing, which emphasised self-control and common sense.

In England, the enlightenment began to lose its appeal with the French Revolution in 1789: the English public was horrified by the atrocities committed by the French on their own citizens. Consequently, the government took steps to avoid a similar revolution in Britain, and it no longer became fashionable to criticise society.

ROMANTICISM: 1798-1870

After all the emphasis on realism and satire, it was only a question of time before the power of the imagination defined a new literary movement.

The Romantic Movement was inspired by the French Revolution, which prompted discussions about freedom, the individual and our place in the world. The Romantics rejected the stylised language of neoclassical literature; instead, they experimented with new ways of expressing themselves. They wanted their literature to be more accessible to a wider range of people, so they included popular forms such as ballads.

As a reaction to the changes in Britain through the Industrial Revolution, many Romantics glorified nature. When reading literature from this period, look out for shepherds, other ordinary people, and idyllic descriptions of mountains, nature and the countryside. Much of the Romantics' writing also has a mystical feel to it and alludes to medieval tales of King Arthur and other myths. Individual imagination was now celebrated and the power of reason downgraded.

There were two generations of the Romantics. The first generation (born roughly 1770-80) includes the artist and poet William Blake as well as William Wordsworth and Samuel Taylor Coleridge, who wrote *Lyrical Ballads* (1798), which could be seen as starting the Romantic period of literature. Other key figures are Sir Walter Scott, Poet Laureate Robert Southey, Charles Lamb and William Hazlitt. The second generation was born just before or in the 1890s. It includes John Keats, Mary Wollstonecraft Shelley, author of *Frankenstein*, her husband Percy Bysshe Shelley, and the notorious Lord Byron. There was also the essayist Thomas De Quincey who, born in 1785, falls between the two generations.

Eventually, the Romantics became victims of their reputation as creative, imaginative thinkers. The world was changing. New writers who could describe its gritty realities were needed.

VICTORIAN PERIOD: 1837-1901

This literary movement covers all literature that was written during the reign of Queen Victoria.

If you enjoy novels, you can thank the Victorians. This was an age where the novel replaced poetry to become the dominant genre.

Charles Dickens was a prolific writer in the first part of this movement. William Thackeray's *Vanity Fair* (1848) was also popular, and other 1840s bestselling novels included the works of Charlotte, Emily and Anne Brontë, who originally published under the male pseudonyms of Currer, Ellis and Acton Bell. Mary Ann Evans published under the pseudonym George Eliot and her novel *Middlemarch* (1872) has been described as probably the greatest novel in the English language. Later in Queen Victoria's reign emerged Thomas Hardy, who was a major novelist and poet.

As we saw with Charles Dickens in the last chapter, Victorian literature uses realism to address concerns about the poor. It also holds a mirror up to life, commenting on morality—consequently, there is not always a happy ending. Robert Browning and Alfred Tennyson were the most famous poets of this age, and Gilbert and Sullivan were celebrated for their comic operas. Popular playwrights included George Bernard Shaw and Oscar Wilde.

MODERNISM: 1910-1941

This period encompasses World War I and part of World War II. These wars, coupled with developments in industrialisation and globalisation, caused many people to question what was happening to the world. Out of these questions emerged Modernism.

Modernist fiction is often quite depressing. Common themes are the decline of civilisation, the alienation of people in a world of machines and capitalism, and loneliness.

To heighten the impact of the writer's emotions, modernist literature was often written in the first person, and the structured stories of Victorian times were replaced by a looser stream of consciousness. Interestingly, like the earlier neo-classicists, modernists often used irony and satire to criticise society. There was also a trend of alluding to other writers' works.

Some famous modernist writers include James Joyce (*Ulysses*), Virginia Woolf (*Mrs Dalloway* and *To the Lighthouse*), D.H. Lawrence (*Lady Chatterley's Lover*) and Samuel Beckett (*Waiting for Godot*).

Others include Joseph Conrad (*Heart of Darkness*), Nobel Prize winner T.S. Eliot (*The Waste Land* and *The Love Song of J. Alfred Prufrock*), William Faulkner (*As I Lay Dying*), John Steinbeck (*Of Mice and Men*), Sylvia Plath (*The Bell Jar*), F. Scott Fitzgerald (*The Great Gatsby*) and William Butler Yeats, the first Irishman to be awarded the Nobel Prize for literature.

POSTMODERNISM: 1941-TODAY

The actual date that the postmodern period began is debatable: some scholars say the 1950s and others the 1960s. Yet more use 1941, which marks the deaths of James Joyce and Virginia Woolf.

While modernists struggled to make sense of the world, postmodernists believe that it is impossible to understand precise meanings behind ideas, concepts or events.

Therefore, the purpose of postmodern literature is to reveal the world's absurdities, countless paradoxes and ironies.

Here are some examples of postmodern stylistic techniques:

Faction: Mixing real historical events with fictional events.

Intertextuality: Referring to other literary works within a piece of writing.

Maximalism: Long, disorganised, highly detailed writing.

Metafiction: Either writing about writing or making readers aware that they are reading a work of fiction.

Minimalism: Common, unexceptional characters and events.

Pastiche: Taking ideas and literary styles from previous writings and pasting them together to create new styles.

Reader Involvement: The writer might address the reader directly, or acknowledge within the writing itself that it is a work of fiction.

Temporal Distortion: Not using linear timelines and narrative techniques. The narrative might be fragmented.

You might have noticed that some of these stylistic techniques are also associated with other literary movements or authors. For example, Charlotte Bronte employs **reader involvement** when, at the end of *Jane Eyre*, she writes 'Reader, I married him'. In the last chapter, we also saw examples of intertextuality used by Jane Austen in *Northanger Abbey*.

It cannot be stressed enough that, as much as we might like to categorise an author and describe how he or she is part of a literary movement, there are always exceptions. After all, the whole point of being creative is to be different.

It will be interesting to see if future scholars categorise today's writers as part of the postmodernist movement.

Other Literary Movements

We have examined the main movements in Britain, but there are others. Some overlap with another period, and others occur abroad. Below are some examples that you might encounter in your studies.

TRANSCENDENTALISM 1836-1860

Transcendentalism is a nineteenth century American literary and philosophical movement that began in Boston, America. It was led by the American essayist, lecturer, and poet Ralph Waldo Emerson and the teacher, writer, philosopher and reformer Amos Bronson Alcott.

Like British Romantics, transcendentalists were nonconformists, believing in the rights of the individual to follow truth, even if it went against established laws or customs. They rejected traditional authority and built a foundation for the abolition of slavery, the civil rights and conscientious objector movements.

Transcendence involves following your intuition to gain a new understanding of the world and your place—as a moral, idealistic person—in it. Emerson promoted the idea of humans having a universal soul, which provides intuition. This was seen as a privileged form of knowledge, more important than intellect.

Emerson wrote essays about transcendentalism; transcendental elements can also be seen in *Walden* by Henry David Thoreau. Other members of the group included Bronson Alcott, Margaret Fuller, F. H. Hedge, Theodore Parker and George Ripley. Transcendentalism influenced Nathaniel Hawthorne *(The Scarlet Letter)*, Herman Melville (*Moby-Dick*) and the poet Walt Whitman.

REALISM 1820-1920

Literary Realism aims to describe things as they actually are, as opposed to in a stylised or romanticised way. As you will see from the dates, Realism coincides with the Victorian and earlier enlightenment periods.

Literary critic Ian Watt in *The Rise of the Novel* (1957) believes that this movement began with the early 18th century novel, with its founding fathers being Daniel Defoe (1660-1731), who wrote *Robinson Crusoe*; Samuel Richardson (1689-1761), most famous for three novels (*Pamela: Or, Virtue Rewarded, Clarissa: Or the History of a Young Lady,* and *The History of Sir Charles Grandison*); and Henry Fielding (1707-1754), author of *Tom Jones* and incidentally founder of London's first police force, the Bow Street Runners.

These novels appealed to a new middle-class reading public, who enjoyed reading realistic descriptions of ordinary people and their relationships with each other.

The Victorian nineteenth century novel *Middlemarch* by George Eliot has been categorised as a work of Realism partly because it describes people's reactions to the Reform Bill of 1832, which gave the vote to more people living in towns; the railways; and developments in medical science.

Realism continued mainly in America and lasted until the end of the nineteenth century. Its popularity began to wane because it was felt that it dwelt too much on the negative side of life. Other criticism came from authors like Henry James, who said that there was too much focus on character and not enough on plot.

NATURALISM 1870-1920

Charles Darwin's theory of evolution influenced naturalistic writers, who believed that a person's environment shaped his or her character.

Both Realism and Naturalism describe things as they are, but naturalism also tries to scientifically analyse what influences a person's actions (i.e. their environment or genes).

Naturalism is another literary movement in which pessimism is a key characteristic. In fact, a criticism of this movement was that it focused too much on vice and misery. The harshness of life and the darker side of human nature are described by the writer in a detached tone. To make things worse, characters do not have the power to change their fate—this is called determinism.

Key writers from this period include Émile Zola, who proclaimed that he was the leader of French Naturalism; Stephen Crane, an American writer, who believed that the writer had a responsibility to analyse; W. D. Howells, Frank Norris and Theodore Dreiser, who wrote about the environment affecting human behaviour. Other practitioners included Jack London, Edith Wharton (*The House of Mirth*) and Ellen Glasgow (*Barren Ground*).

EXISTENTIALISM 1850-today

In existentialist philosophy, there is no God: the idea is that we are isolated in a chaotic world, coming from nothing and moving towards nothing. Consequently, there's no purpose for us being on Earth and no explanation as to why we exist— therefore, our existence is absurd. The only way that we can come to terms with this is by embracing life.

Existentialists believe that because we live in a chaotic world, we can choose to do anything we like. This places a heavy burden of responsibility on us, as we have to make choices based on what we personally believe is right; however, we should not unthinkingly do what is expected of us. We have to define our own meaning in life and try to make rational decisions despite living in an irrational universe.

The philosophy's roots lie in the 19th century with the philosophers Søren Kierkegaard and Friedrich Nietzsche. In the early 20th century, writers and philosophers around the world explored existentialist ideas. Key figures included Lev Shestov and Nikolai Berdyaev in Russia; Gabriel Marcel and Jean Wahl in France; Karl Jaspers, Martin Heidegger, and Martin Buber in Germany; and José Ortega y Gasset and Miguel de Unamuno y Jugo in Spain.

As a literary movement, existentialism peaked in France after World War II, spearheaded by two famous French writers, Jean-Paul Sartre and Albert Camus. Sartre's books about existentialism include *Being and Nothingness* and *Existentialism and Humanism*. Common themes in existential literature are dread, boredom, alienation, nothingness, the absurd, commitment and freedom. Sartre's famous works of fiction include *The Age of Reason, No Exit, Nausea* and *The Wall* while Camus's best works include *The Fall, The Stranger* and *The Plague*. Maurice Merleau-Ponty and Sartre's partner the feminist Simone de Beauvoir were also internationally famous existentialists. The latter wrote about feminist and existential ethics in *The Second Sex* and *The Ethics of Ambiguity*.

In the twenty-first century, you might read a text with combined elements of existentialism and postmodernism.

THE BLOOMSBURY GROUP 1912-1940s

Not quite fitting the Victorian or modernist literary movements, the small and informal Bloomsbury Group contained roughly a dozen artists, writers and politicians, who lived or worked in Bloomsbury in central London. The friends often met to share their thoughts about a range of subjects.

They agreed with the philosopher George Edward Moore, who stated that you don't have to prove to other people that an idea or feeling is right and good. The Bloomsbury Group applied this concept (called 'intrinsic worth') to their discussions.

Their ideas about society were radical and shocking for the time. They questioned the tradition of monogamous marriage: some had open sexual relationships with each other, and they did not criticise homosexuality. Naturally, the tabloid press had a field day publishing stories about their unconventional relationships.

The group also revelled in criticising the establishment. They passionately voiced their views about world peace and social issues, and some members led anti-war movements.

If the group had a leader, it was the feminist, novelist and essayist Virginia Woolf. Other members included her brothers Adrian and Thoby Stephen; sister Vanessa Stephen Bell and brother-in-law Clive Bell; her husband, Leonard Woolf; and critic and biographer Giles Lytton Stratchey, famous for *Landmarks of French Literature* and *Eminent Victorians*. Later, the novelist E. M. Forster (*A Passage to India*) joined the group. The noted economist John Maynard Keynes was also a member.

In 1917, Woolf and her husband founded a publishing company called the Hogarth Press, which supported writers such as T.S. Eliot.

The group began to decline in the 1930s when its members began to die, and Virginia Woolf drowned herself in 1941.

THE BEAT GENERATION 1950s-60s

The Beat Generation, also called the Beat Movement, is an American social and literary movement that originated in the bohemian artist communities of San Francisco, Los Angeles and New York City's Greenwich Village.

The word *beat* meant exhausted and beaten down. It also meant beatific or blessed. Many members were jazz fans, so the word *beat* also had musical connotations. Members of the movement called themselves **beatniks** to emphasise their lack of conformity.

Unlike the Bloomsbury Group, they were not interested in politics or social problems. Instead, their focus was on individual freedom. They meditated or used drugs to cultivate mystical experiences and, rejecting the idea of conformity, they dressed and spoke in nonconformist ways.

It is only to be expected that their literature rejected a formal, impersonal style: the defining feature of their writing was its impression of spontaneity and improvisation. For this reason, a lot of Beat poetry was performance-based and read in public to jazz accompaniment.

Key Beat writers include William Burroughs, Gregory Corso, Lawrence Ferlinghetti, Allen Ginsberg, John Clellon Holmes, Jack Kerouac, Philip Whalen, and Gary Snyder.

The movement lost its popularity in the 1960s.

What Next?

In this chapter, we have visited some of the literary movements that might have influenced your writers' choices of style and theme. When you are reading a text, look for clues with language, style and theme that might link it to a particular movement. Then use these to stimulate your research and wider reading so that you can discuss the extent to which your writer shares characteristics with the literary period.

The final aspect of context is the writer's choice of genre, which we will explore in the next chapter.

Chapter 10

AO3: Genre

Although genre can be defined as a category of writing, the boundaries between genre and literary form are sometimes blurred. A short story is an example of literary form, but some people classify it as a genre because it became extremely popular during the Victorian literary movement. Furthermore, many Victorian short stories contain elements of ghost stories, thereby blending genres.

The overlapping of genres is common: you might be reading a text that is a subgroup of a genre or a mixture of genres. Shakespeare's plays are **comedies** (light-hearted plays with happy endings and marriages); **tragedies** (stressful situations, ending in death); and **histories** (plays based on actual historical characters and events). Later in his life, Shakespeare experimented with a new genre, the **tragicomedy**, which blended elements of tragedy and comedy.

If genre classification systems sound confusing, don't let this worry you: your analysis is more important. Consider the writer's technique and tone of writing, choice of subject matter and character.

Also consider what might have influenced writers to employ a particular genre. Ask yourself the extent to which they conform to the genre. What effects are they trying to achieve? To what extent are they successful? Finally, what is the impact on you, the reader?

Popular genres today include **action, adventure, crime, horror, romance and thrillers**. Some of these (for example, romance) are timeless.

The aim of this chapter is to introduce you to key literary genres. Use them as a starting point for your research; this is not an exhaustive list and there are many others.

Allegory

You might remember that an allegory is a type of extended metaphor, which has an obvious surface meaning and also a symbolic meaning beneath the text. A famous example is George Orwell's *Animal Farm*, which is an allegory of the 1917 Russian Revolution and the early years of communism.

Comedy

Comedy was one of just two dramatic genres (the second being **tragedy**) more than 2,000 years ago in Greece. The word **comedy** means 'revelry' or 'merry-making', as it originates from a festival that was dedicated to Dionysus, the Greek god of wine and revelry.

Comedies appear in different literary forms, but they do share some characteristics. These include:

The theme of **love** or strong physical attraction, which is a motivating force.

Characters as caricatures. These might be an old man, who is in love with a young girl; a young girl, who rejects the advances of the old man in favour of a young man; or a young girl, who has to choose between two young men; a young man, who has to fight to win the young girl's love; an incompetent freeloading friend, who creates problems for the young man; and a servant, who is cleverer than his master.

Plain, everyday **speech**, with lots of **puns** and wordplay, including **double entendre** (a word with two meanings, the second of which is deliberately rude).

A **structure** aptly summarised in Todorov's Narrative Theory (see chapter 12), which of course results in a **happy ending**.

In the 16th and 17th centuries, Puritanism and the Civil War in England put a stop to comedies performed on stage. From 1649 when King Charles II ascended the throne, comedy became popular again. A new genre called **Restoration Comedy** emerged at this time.

Following two world wars, the genre of comedy changed in the 20th century. The focus now became the decay and disintegration of society. Black comedy, containing dark and depressing themes, emerged as a subgenre, as did absurdist comedy with its surreal humour.

Popular examples of bestselling prose in this genre include Douglas Adams's *The Hitchhiker's Guide to the Galaxy* (1995), Joseph Heller's *Catch-22* (2004) and any of the Terry Pratchett's *Discworld* series, which can also be categorised as fantasy.

Dystopian Genre

A **dystopia** is an imaginary place where life is extremely bad (its opposite is **utopia**). Dystopian literature is sometimes classified as **futuristic** because settings are often in the future. The author uses this genre to make a social comment on the consequences of a particular scientific, social or political ideology. For example, both Aldous Huxley's *Brave New World* (1931) and George Orwell's *Nineteen Eighty-Four* (1949) reflect contemporary fears of living under a socialist regime where independent thinking is forbidden. Huxley also imagines the impact that advances of science and technology have on individual lives. Margaret Atwood's *The Handmaid's Tale* (1985) takes human rights abuses and imagines a future society in which these all come together.

Fantasy

Stories in the fantasy genre are often set in an imaginary world (often medieval), and they contain magic and magical creatures. George MacDonald is believed to have written the first modern fantasy novel, but J.R.R. Tolkien firmly established this genre with *The Hobbit* (1937) and its sequel *The Lord of the Rings* (1954-5). Inspired by Old Germanic stories and mythology, Tolkien reworked ideas from Anglo-Saxon and Norse literature such as slaying a dragon that is guarding treasure. Today, George R.R. Martin's *Game of Thrones* series is the most popular example of the fantasy genre for adults.

Gothic

The origins of this genre, which is dominated by the sub-genre Gothic horror, lie in Horace Walpole's *The Castle of Otranto* (1764) which, in its second edition, was subtitled *A Gothic Story*. The Gothic genre combines Romanticism with fiction and horror. In Gothic literature, characters usually include a virtuous orphaned heroine (who faints a lot) and a murderous villain with terrifying eyes. Tales are set in the past, often in remote foreign castles or monasteries with secret subterranean passages. Expect to encounter a vampire, ghost or monster. The weather's usually horrible and there will be a lot of melodrama.

This genre was popular in the Romantic Movement but, by the 1840s, it began to decline. It did, however, revive in a Victorian craze for ghost stories, and this evolved into the sub-genre of Victorian Gothic.

The Gothic genre retains its popularity today, inspiring other sub-genres such as Southern Gothic (set in America's south), and Gothic Science Fiction, which has the same atmosphere as Gothic novels, but uses science to explain Gothic elements; for example, a vampire might be the result of a contagion. Therefore science explains the existence of vampires.

Historical

This genre is quite obviously set in the past and has a historical backdrop. For example, Markus Zusak's *The Book Thief* (2005) is set in Nazi Germany; Philippa Gregory's *The Other Boleyn Girl* (2001) is set in the reign of Henry VIII; and Arthur Golden's *Memoirs of a Geisha* (1997) is set in Kyoto, Japan, before and after World War II.

Magical Realism

This genre is not part of the British literary heritage, but it's good to be aware of significant genres from other countries. If you enjoy the fantasy genre, magical realism is for you.

Originating in Latin America, the roots of magical realism lie in the Roman Catholic religion, whose followers believe in miracles. In the literature of magical realism, this idea is extended to the idea of magic being possible and a normal part of everyday life.

Perhaps one the most famous South American authors to write in this genre is Gabriel Garcia Marquez, who won the Nobel Prize for Literature in 1982. His best-selling *One Hundred Years of Solitude* (1967) contains miraculous events, which are regarded as commonplace occurrences. Another award-winning author is Isabel Allende, who wrote various magical realism novels, perhaps the most famous being *The House of the Spirits* (1982).

Mystery

This genre usually contains a crime that needs to be solved and sometimes a death (in which case, it would cross over to the murder-mystery genre). There's often a detective who solves the crime; the suspects all have a motive and opportunity. The mystery might also be supernatural—this was the theme of popular pulp magazines in the 1930s and 1940s.

Interestingly, the mystery genre emerged about 200 years ago when police forces were established and there was a clear need for detectives. Famous literary works include *The Murders in the Rue Morgue* by Edgar Allan Poe (1841); *The Moonstone* by Wilkie Collins (1868); and the hugely popular Sherlock Holmes mysteries, written by Sir Arthur Conan Doyle. In the 1920s, Edward Stratemeyer wrote the *Hardy Boys* and *Nancy Drew* (under pseudonyms), and Agatha Christie emerged as a celebrated author with her famous detectives Hercule Poirot and Miss Marple. She published more than eighty works in her lifetime, including *Murder on the Orient Express*

(1934) and the best selling mystery novel of all time *And Then There Were None* (1939).

Romance

This genre spans hundreds of years. It was popular in the medieval literary movement, featuring wizards and dragons, and knights rescuing maidens in distress.

In the 17th century, it began to decline in popularity due to the Enlightenment period's fashion of rationalism. Later in the 18th century, it re-emerged as part of the Romantic Movement, splitting into the subgenres of Gothic romance and historical romance.

Typical characteristics of the romance genre are that two people fall in love with each other, there's an obstacle, they overcome the obstacle, and they live happily ever after.

Science Fiction

This genre is set in an imaginary future and—unlike dystopian literature—the future is not necessarily bad. The emphasis is on real or imaginary scientific discoveries and space technology such as time travel, space travel and parallel universes. French author Jules Verne is considered the father of science fiction. Examples of his work include *Journey to the Centre of the Earth* (1864) and *Twenty Thousand Leagues under the Sea* (1870). The British author H. G. Wells wrote *The Time Machine* (1895), *The Island of Doctor Moreau* (1896), *The Invisible Man* (1897) and *The War of the Worlds* (1898). This genre is still popular today.

Social or Political Novels

The social novel is a work of fiction that aims to draw attention to a social problem. This might be poverty, child labour, prejudice or violence. As we have seen, many of Charles Dickens's novels contain a social message. Other examples include *Mary Barton* (1848) by Elizabeth Gaskell, who focuses on relations between employers and factory workers, and *Shirley* (1849) by Charlotte Brontë, which is set against the backdrop of the Luddite uprisings.

Tragedy

Greek playwrights established this genre more than 2,000 years ago. As we have seen, at the time there were just two dramatic genres: **comedy** and **tragedy**. The word **tragedy** means 'goat song' and links to goats being sacrificed at public festivals.

Traditionally, the protagonist of a tragedy is a high-ranking person, who faces a loss due a weakness in his character. In Shakespeare's *Hamlet*, Hamlet the prince dies because he wants to avenge himself against his step-father, who murdered his father. Even though his desire for revenge is understandable, the fact that he takes it into his own hands is seen to be his weakness.

Shakespeare further developed the genre, making protagonists (like Romeo and Juliet) ordinary people. He also presented circumstances as being responsible for deaths rather than personal weaknesses. In addition, he developed the moralistic theme of sinners gaining their true deserts; for example, Macbeth dies as a consequence of murdering King Duncan.

In modern times, the tragic genre might contain a message about the failings of society. Arthur Miller's *The Crucible* (1953) appears to be about the 1692-3 Salem witch trials in America; in reality, it's an allegory of McCarthyism, a campaign led by Senator Joseph McCarthy in 1950-4. In this campaign, the American government accused people, many of them innocent, of being communists and then blacklisted them, firing them from their jobs.

Like dramatic tragedies, tragic novels deal with tragic themes. For example, *Tess of the D'Urbervilles* (1891) by Thomas Hardy focuses on the negative consequences of sexual double-standards.

SUMMARY

It's important to remember that the genres detailed in this chapter are examples only: there are many more, including sub-genres. When you are reading a text, it might also contain elements of at least two genres.

At the end of this guide is an example essay in which knowledge of context, including literary tradition and genre, is woven into the analysis.

Chapter 11

AO4: Exploring Connections

AO4 requires you to:

Explore connections across literary texts.

This means that you are assessed on your ability to explore similarities and differences between texts.

The number of texts that you compare in an essay will depend upon the exam board that you are following; your teacher will provide you with further information. The length of your essay will also vary, depending upon the specification of the respective exam board.

Of course, you will be doing more than simply summarising the similarities and differences: for your comparison to illuminate the reader, you should consider:

1. How apparent differences are similar.

2. How apparent similarities are significantly different.

3. How your core texts are framed by a broader network of texts (wider reading).

4. How your core texts are framed by a broader network of contexts. In the case of drama, for example, these might be the perceptions of modern and contemporary audiences.

5. How your core texts are framed by a broader network of critical responses, which you could also compare.

The skill of comparing texts is a challenging one for many students, especially if the essay is a long one. Some students find the task of writing lengthy essays daunting, and they lose their thread of discussion in long, rambling responses. To avoid this, it's essential that you plan your ideas.

Planning

First, brainstorm your ideas and link them to the question. What are the similarities and differences between the texts? Work out your thesis statement (a sentence with one main idea or point that you will develop in your essay).

If you are not sure about what to compare, useful starting points are ideas about the main theme(s). You could explore attitudes and values, characterisation, tone, setting and mood, the extent to which the texts conform to their literary movements or genres, and the writers' choices of structure, form and language to convey particular ideas. You would also analyse critical responses to the texts (see chapter 12).

Each student has a preferred method of planning: some like spider diagrams while other prefer bullet point lists. Whichever method you use, I would recommend including the following:

1. The title of your essay. This might sound obvious, but many students stray from the question simply because they digress and lose their thread of discussion. Keeping the question in front of you should help you to focus on the key words.

2. Underline or highlight the key words so that you maintain your focus and consistently tailor your response to them.

3. Write down the assessment objectives that are being assessed and their weightings. This will help you to keep them firmly in mind and to integrate them into your plan.

EXAMPLE STRUCTURE OF A PLAN

Title of task:

Compare the presentation and consequences of love in [text A] and [text B].

AOs & Percentage of Essay Mark:

AO1 – 20% (detailed understanding, writing skills and terminology)

AO2 – 20% (language, form, structure, analytical methods, quoting)

AO3 – 20% (context)

AO4 – 20% (exploring connections)

AO5 – 20% (exploring different readings or ways of reading the texts)

Plan

NB: You will probably not refer to every AO in every paragraph, so adapt the following plan to your needs.

EXAMPLE THEME PER PARAGRAPH	POINTS	
Introduction	AO3 & thesis statement.	
Presentation of love: comparison (AO4) of infatuation & consequences	**Text 1** AO1 terminology: AO2: AO3: AO5:	**Text 2** AO1 terminology: AO2: AO3: AO5:
Presentation of love: comparison (AO4) of religious/spiritual & consequences	**Text 1** AO1 terminology: AO2: AO3: AO5:	**Text 2** AO1 terminology: AO2: AO3: AO5:
Presentation of love: comparison (AO4) of romantic & consequences	**Text 1** AO1 terminology: AO2: AO3: AO5:	**Text 2** AO1 terminology: AO2: AO3: AO5:
Presentation of love: comparison (AO4) of	**Text 1**	**Text 2**

physical & consequences	AO1 terminology: AO2: AO3: AO5:	AO1 terminology: AO2: AO3: AO5:
Conclusion	Summarise thoughts	

The above example is an illustration of how you might organise your ideas whilst bearing the AOs in mind. Obviously, you would need a lot more space in your plan! You might even have to add an extra column for a third text.

Introduction

This might also sound rather obvious, but you would be surprised by how many students forget to write the authors and titles of the texts that they are comparing in the introduction.

Once you have introduced the texts, refer to them in subsequent paragraphs by the surnames of the writers; some titles are very long and, if you repeat them in every paragraph, your thread of discussion will become slow and cumbersome, affecting your AO1 mark.

You will also need to include information about the purpose of the comparison. Do NOT write...

Bad Introduction:

In this essay, I am going to compare *Macbeth* by William Shakespeare with *Great Expectations* by Charles Dickens.

As well as being boring, the above example does not contain a thesis statement. Review chapter 5 if necessary, as you need to include a thesis statement in your introduction. A better introduction would be...

Better Introduction:

Both Macbeth in William Shakespeare's *Macbeth* and Pip in Charles Dickens's *Great Expectations* have the ambition to rise in class. In both texts, the protagonists are so blinded by their ambitions that they do not see the consequences of their actions.

The above introduction is rather brief and chapter 5 contains ideas about how to expand your ideas. It introduces the texts, however, and it contains a clear thesis statement.

When you have planned your ideas, you need to decide how you are going to structure your comparisons in the writing process. There are two approaches.

Structuring Content

ALTERNATING (OR POINT-BY-POINT) METHOD

This method has a clear theme of comparison per paragraph. Each paragraph contains:

- A comparative topic sentence

- Discussion of first text

- Discussion of second text with comparisons to the first text

This method is then repeated throughout your essay until you arrive at your conclusion. In the example below, the three sections have been highlighted.

Alternating Method: Example Paragraph

While **both** Macbeth and Pip share an ambition to rise, this is facilitated by external factors. Macbeth may have been content with his new title of the 'Thane of Cawdor' had he not met the witches, who prophesised that he would be 'King' (Act I, Scene III). When she reads his letter, Lady Macbeth becomes the ambitious driving force in her famous soliloquy (Act I, Scene V) when she calls on the 'spirits' to 'unsex' her as a woman so that she has the necessary male resolve to plan regicide. The contemporary audience was more religious than a modern audience and the crime of regicide would have been more heinous: it was believed that God gave the King power and so opposing the King was the same as opposing God. In those deeply religious times, this was considered sacrilege, the worst sin of all.[1] In Dickens's novel, **however**, Pip is the unwitting catalyst of his transformation into a 'gentleman' when he helps the escaped convict Magwitch. Although he has the desire to rise in life ('I wished Joe had been rather more genteelly brought up, and then I should have been so too'), the means to rise are absent until he has a 'secret benefactor'. **Unlike** Macbeth, who actively stabs King Duncan, Pip is a passive recipient. Nevertheless, **both** Macbeth and Pip have chance encounters, which change their lives completely.

---

[1]BBC Bitesize *Macbeth: Background* (2014)
http://www.bbc.co.uk/bitesize/higher/english/macbeth/background/revision/1/ [accessed 12th April, 2015]

COMMENTARY

The topic sentence introduces the comparative theme of the paragraph. The comparing and contrasting discourse markers are in **bold.** As Macbeth is discussed first and Pip second, this order of discussion would continue throughout the essay. Note that there is roughly an equal amount of writing for each text: you should not allow one text to dominate. The summative comparative sentence at the end of the paragraph concludes your thoughts.

BLOCK METHOD

With the block method, your essay is structured in the following way:

1. Introduction

2. A very long paragraph with your points about the first text

3. A very long paragraph with your points about the second text, in which you would make comparisons

4. Conclusion

WHICH METHOD SHOULD I CHOOSE?

The block method works well with short essays, but it poses potential pitfalls for A' level essays:

- There might be a lot of space between the points you make in your text A paragraph and the points that you make in your text B paragraph. Therefore, you or your reader might forget what you are actually comparing when you come to your text B paragraph.

- Some students list everything about text A and then everything about text B, but they don't compare.

- Some students might compare only in the conclusion when they should have compared throughout.

I always recommend the **alternating method**, as it helps you to focus on the key words of the question and make consistently detailed comparisons. It also works particularly well with longer essays.

Discourse Markers

In chapter 5, we reviewed a range of discourse markers to signpost your thread of discussion. Below are ones that focus on comparing and contrasting ideas:

COMPARING IDEAS

As well as...,...

Both...

Each of...

In the same way,

Just as...so

Like...,...

Neither...

Similarly,

The same...

INTRODUCING CONTRASTING IDEAS

Although...

Conversely,

However,

In contrast,

Alternatively,

Nevertheless,

Despite this,

On the one hand,... but on the other hand,...

On the other hand,...

Unlike...,...

Whereas...,...

While...

While there is evidence that...

Yet...

Conclusion

Some students write beautifully crafted essays and them forget to summarise their thoughts in relation to their thesis statement in their conclusion. Don't be one of those students! Revise conclusions in chapter 5 if necessary.

Finally...

Although we have explored ways to focus on the assessment objectives when planning a comparative essay, we have only briefly alluded to assessment objective 5.

It's now time to examine the final AO: how to approach different interpretations of texts.

Chapter 12

AO5: Different Interpretations

Assessment Objective 5 requires you to:

Explore literary texts informed by different interpretations.

You are required to demonstrate your knowledge of different interpretations and use them to explore your texts.

Different interpretations can be defined as **different ways of reading a text.** These are many and varied as we shall see below.

Critical Reviews

The most obvious starting point is critics. Your school library might subscribe to a literary journal and your teacher should be able to recommend other resources such as an online database. Do some research and look for articles that are relevant to your essay. You could also source articles on the internet, but you need to be aware that you're looking for quality criticism: a serious academic source will hold more weight than a tweet.

If you agree with a critic's point, explain in detail why you agree. Personally, I always recommend that you look for something to quote and disagree with, as this gives you the opportunity to showcase your critical skills.

Your Interpretation

When you write an essay, remember that you do not have to agree with the question. Even if you have one paragraph that expresses an opposite point of view, you are demonstrating your critical skills.

Performed Versions

You could also explore your text through film and stage versions. The director would be showcasing his or her interpretation of the text, and you would respond to this.

Schools of Literary Theory

There are many school of literary theory, which help to further our understanding and interpretations of texts. Below is an introduction to some key theories. Note that it is not intended to be a definitive list, and your teacher might recommend others.

MARXIST THEORY

Inspired by the philosopher and socialist Karl Marx, Marxist theory examines attitudes to social class and class differences. Marxists are particularly interested in the interactions between the classes. If there is class conflict, Marxists focus on how the lower classes are oppressed and how those in power maintain their power. Marxist literary theory is therefore interested in the negative implications of a capitalist society.

PSYCHOANALYTICAL THEORY

This is based on Freud's theory that we repress our desires by controlling our conscious thought. In literature, a psychoanalytical literary analysis would focus on a character's desires and other psychological states such as any emotional conflict between characters, Oedipal dynamics (boy wants to kill father in order to sleep with mother), etc.

FEMINIST THEORY

The starting point of this theory is that we live in a patriarchal society (a society that men dominate) so, as men have written most of the literature,

men have created their own versions of women.

As a result of this, feminists focus on exploring how women are presented and also the balance of power between men and women. An interesting strain of feminist literary theory is **écriture feminine**, which originated in France in the 1970s and means 'women's writing'. Écriture feminine is written from the position of the female body (marginalised under Freud's theories), using a range of metaphors.

POSTCOLONIAL THEORY

This literary theory explores power and how it combines with other elements like economics. It focuses on how European capitalists from colonial times have exploited those of other races or ethnicities, exploring injustice and oppression, examining how the colonised have been misrepresented in literature because of prejudice.

STRUCTURALIST THEORY

Structuralists see the world of literature as interconnected language, which is part of a larger structure that links to everything that we do, think, feel and see. They look for patterns in plot, structure, language, character and setting, and they examine how these create meaning. They also consider how the text conforms to the conventions of these patterns. Key structuralists include:

Roland Barthes

Barthes proposed that every narrative is interwoven with multiple codes. He believed that what we find in a text depends on our culture, as the different cultural backgrounds of different readers predispose them to notice and interpret different things. Barthes's five codes are:

Enigma code: elements within a text that are not fully explained and create intrigue for the reader.

Action code: the way that action is sequenced, adding suspense.

Semantic code: additional meanings created through the connotations of words.

Symbolic code: additional meanings created through symbolism. This includes binary opposites, which be expressed through character, action and setting.

Cultural code: anything in the text that refers to common bodies of knowledge such as scientific, religious, mythological or historical.

Gustav Freytag

Gustav Freytag was a 19th century German novelist, who created a **pyramid** to illustrate common patterns in the plots of Greek and Shakespearean dramas. Although the pyramid initially applied to five-act plays, it can also be used to analyse short stories and novels.

A summary of his pyramid is on the next page.

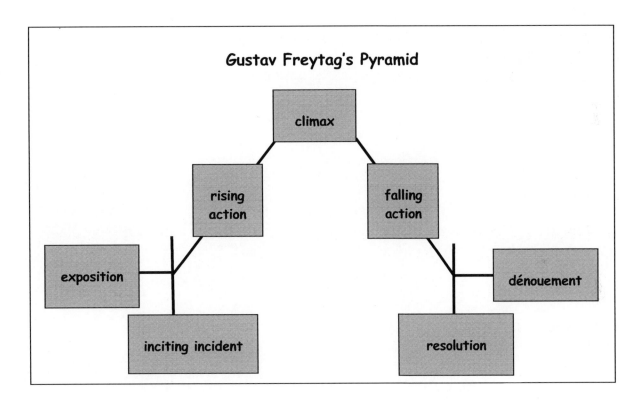

Exposition: the first part of a plot, in which the audience learns about the characters and setting.

Inciting incident (sometimes called **complication**): something happens to begin the action or conflict.

Rising action: the story becomes more exciting as conflicts build.

Climax: The point of greatest tension in a play. The main character comes face-to-face with the conflict and often needs to make a choice.

Falling action: as a result of the climax, there are more events, but we know that the story will soon end.

Resolution: the main problem or conflict is solved.

Dénouement: the fallout: any leftover questions, mysteries or secrets are solved.

Claude Lévi-Strauss

Lévi-Strauss believed that **binary opposites** form the basic structure of all human cultures, and so they reveal a lot about what we think. Binary opposites are words with opposite meanings, for example, 'rough' and 'smooth'. In each pair, one concept is more favoured than the other. For example, 'smooth' is better than 'rough', 'God' is better than the 'devil' and 'love' is better than 'hate'.

Vladimir Propp

Propp was a Russian scholar, who analysed the narrative structure of Russian folk (or fairy) tales. He developed the theory that in every narrative there are particular types of character. For example:

The hero: is on a quest or tries to solve a mystery.

The villain: is in conflict with the hero.

Princess/her father: gives a task to the hero, identifies the false hero, princess marries the hero. (Propp noted that the functions of the princess and the father cannot be clearly distinguished.)

The dispatcher: sends the hero off.

The helper: the hero's sidekick, who sometimes provides comic relief.

The donor: gives the hero something that will help him (or her) complete the quest.

The false hero: claims to be the hero in order to take the hero's place.

Propp also identified 31 **narratemes**, which are narrative units of events that structure a narrative. Stories do not have to contain all of the narratemes:

120

1. A member of family leaves home and a hero is introduced.

2. The hero is warned not to do something.

3. The hero ignores the warning.

4. A villain appears.

5. The villain gains information, which he may use against the hero.

6. The villain attempts to trick a victim.

7. The villain fools the victim/hero.

8. The villain harms someone.

9. The hero learns about a misfortune.

10. The hero decides on counteraction.

11. The hero leaves home.

12. The hero is tested.

13. The hero responds to a donor's test.

14. The hero receives a magical agent.

15. The hero arrives at a new location.

16. The hero and villain fight.

17. The hero is injured.

18. The villain is defeated.

19. Resolution.

20. The hero goes home.

21. The hero is pursued.

22. The hero is rescued.

23. The unrecognised hero arrives home.

24. A false hero claims the hero's success.

25. A difficult task is set.

26. The hero performs the task.

27. The hero is recognised.

28. The false hero is exposed.

29. The hero is acknowledged (e.g. transformed by being given new clothes).

30. The villain is punished.

31. The hero marries and ascends the throne.

Tordorov

Tzvetan Todorov is a Bulgarian philosopher, who states that most stories or plot lines follow the same pattern. These are illustrated below.

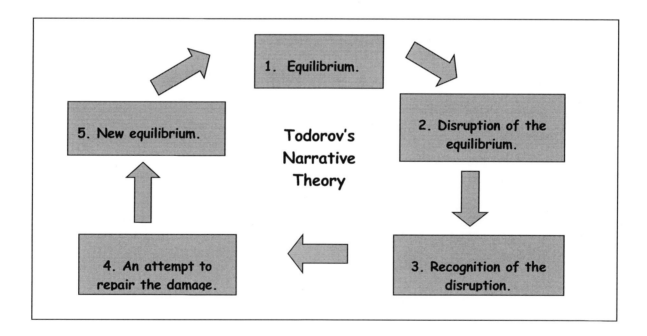

Equilibrium: normal life where everyone is content.

Disruption of the equilibrium: something arises that disrupts this.

122

Recognition of the equilibrium: everyone realises that there is a problem.

An attempt to repair the damage: people try and solve the problem.

New equilibrium: the problem is solved and normal life can resume.

POST-STRUCTURALIST THEORY

Post-structuralists reject the idea that we can analyse literature through structure, as they believe that a text can have more than one meaning. The reader's interpretation is seen to be more important than the author's intentions (interestingly, Barthes with his essay *Death of an Author* moved towards post-structuralism later in life). Post-structuralists believe that readers create new and individual interpretation of a text, which might be influenced by their age, gender, class and race.

POSTMODERNIST THEORY

We are currently living in the postmodern literary period. Postmodernists mix genres, experiment with new structures, have unreliable narrators, paradoxes and fragmented narratives. For more details, see the **postmodern literary movement** in chapter 9.

Literary Theory: Example Responses

The first example response analyses the end of *An Inspector Calls* by J.B. Priestley, using Freytag's Pyramid.

The analysis explores how and why Priestley deviates from Freytag's Pyramid. The points are linked to audience expectations and how Priestley uses structure to heighten tension, create an impact on the audience and spread his message of socialism.

The highlighted words and phrases in **bold** signpost the **analysis** of the text in relation to Freytag's Pyramid. If the writer were simply to identify structural features, this would be feature spotting, which would result in very few marks.

Example 1:

Priestley **deviates** from the structural features of Freytag's Pyramid at the end of *An Inspector Calls*. At the end of Act 3, **we expect** the dénouement to be the learning process of Sheila and Eric, who have changed, and the complacency of the Birlings and Gerald Croft, who have not changed. However, the tension suddenly rockets with an unexpected climax at the end of the play when the phone rings; **after this climax, there is no falling action, resolution or dénouement.** The characters are plunged into chaos when the climactic curtain falls on the news that a girl has died and a real inspector is on his way. Priestley decides to end the play in this fashion **in order to encourage the audience** to think about the Inspector's identity, his socialist philosophy, and our responsibility to others. **A traditional dénouement would not have been such an effective device: ending on a climax encouraged the audience to take the play and its message about socialism home with them.**

The next example is a student's response to critic Maurice Richardson and his interpretation of *Dracula* by Bram Stocker.

Example 2:

Maurice Richardson believes that there is more to *Dracula* than it being simply a gothic horror novel, written to thrill. Despite the gothic conventions of the remote setting with a 'vast ruined castle', the 'heavy, oppressive sense of thunder' and—perhaps **to the modern reader**—the cliché of 'the wolves', which 'began to howl as though the moonlight had some peculiar effect on them', the novel can be interpreted in another way. **Richardson analyses 'Dracula' from a Freudian perspective, stating that** the vampire represents repressed sexuality[1]. He states that Lucy and other vampire females are killed by stakes, which he interprets as phallic symbols. **Victorians are known for** their emotional inhibitions and their factually uninformed views of sex (a well-known story is that of a mother, who counselled her newly-married

---

[1] Maurice Richardson, *The Psychoanalysis of Ghost Stories,* (Twentieth Century, 1959), pp. 419-431.

...Continued

daughter to lie back and think of England).[2] The stake therefore represents the dominant male impaling a passive female; **however, if we examine the broader social and political context, we can take our analysis beyond the sexual. For example,** women had no political voice in a patriarchal society in which all the laws were made and passed by men. **From a feminist perspective, perhaps the stake could symbolise the political power**—or the rod of iron rule—that men wielded over women. **Moreover,** women had few legal rights to protect them: it was only in 1839 that children under the age of seven could stay with their mother if their parents separated; only in 1857 that women could divorce husbands for cruelty or desertion; only in 1870 that women were allowed to keep any money that they earned; and only in 1891 that unhappily married women could no longer be forced to live with their husbands.[3] **The stake could therefore symbolise the legal power that husbands held over women** and the economic powers of a patriarchal society in which there were limited opportunities for separated or divorced married women to work and support not only themselves but their dependants.

---

[2]*Sex and Sexuality in the 19th Century* (London: Victoria & Albert Museum, n.d.),
http://www.vam.ac.uk/content/articles/s/sex-and-sexuality-19th-century/ [accessed 3 May, 2015].

[3]*Womens Rights* [sic], (History learning Site, 2000),
http://www.historylearningsite.co.uk/womensrights.htm [accessed 3 May, 2015].

COMMENTARY

The sections highlighted in **red** signpost the thread of discussion. Richardson's view is introduced, contextualised against the conventions of the Gothic genre and referenced against an interpretation of a modern reader. Details of Richardson's Freudian (or psychoanalytical) analysis are then presented. Richardson's view is stated by the student, who responds by referring to her research into Victorian attitudes to sex. She then demonstrates her own critical view by proposing two symbolic interpretations of the stake. The first is informed by her knowledge of the political and legal context while the second applies feminist methodology.

With the third footnote, you will see the word [sic]. This means that the word or phrase immediately before it is exactly how it appears in the original. (*Womens Rights* should be written as *Women's Rights* with an apostrophe of possession.)

Finally...

In this guide to A' level literature, you have been presented with many examples to illustrate the assessment objectives. Whatever you do, never allow literary theory to dominate: your informed voice and views are the most important.

On the next page is a bonus chapter, which contains an example essay. The aim of the essay is to illustrate how to integrate the assessment objectives into your writing.

BONUS CHAPTER: EXAMPLE ESSAY!

This special bonus chapter provides a detailed analysis of Andrew Marvell's poem *To His Coy Mistress*, which is printed below.

Read the poem and then the response. The essay highlights the methods that Marvell has used, states their effects and explains why they might have been chosen. You might find it useful to identify the relevant AOs and analyse how the writer explores meaning in the poem.

Note that AO4 (exploring connections) is not assessed, just as you will not always be assessed on every single assessment objective. Your teacher should advise you on this.

Although the essay is written in the style of a non-exam assessed piece and uses footnotes, it does not contain a bibliography: you already have an example of how to write one in chapter 6.

Please note that for copyright reasons I have been unable to quote some of my sources of information and have summarised them instead. In a non-exam assessed essay, you would be expected to quote your wider reading and drop it into your sentences.

In an essay written for an exam, quoting or referencing your wider reading would be sufficient.

To His Coy Mistress

By Andrew Marvell

Had we but world enough and time,

This coyness, lady, were no crime.

We would sit down, and think which way

To walk, and pass our long love's day.

Thou by the Indian Ganges' side

Shouldst rubies find; I by the tide

Of Humber would complain. I would

Love you ten years before the flood,

And you should, if you please, refuse

Till the conversion of the Jews.

My vegetable love should grow

Vaster than empires and more slow;

An hundred years should go to praise

Thine eyes, and on thy forehead gaze;

Two hundred to adore each breast,

But thirty thousand to the rest;

An age at least to every part,

And the last age should show your heart.

For, lady, you deserve this state,

Nor would I love at lower rate.

But at my back I always hear

Time's wingèd chariot hurrying near;

And yonder all before us lie

Deserts of vast eternity.

Thy beauty shall no more be found;

Nor, in thy marble vault, shall sound

My echoing song; then worms shall try

That long-preserved virginity,

And your quaint honour turn to dust,

And into ashes all my lust;

The grave's a fine and private place,

But none, I think, do there embrace.

Now therefore, while the youthful hue

Sits on thy skin like morning dew,

And while thy willing soul transpires

At every pore with instant fires,

Now let us sport us while we may,

And now, like amorous birds of prey,

Rather at once our time devour

Than languish in his slow-chapped power.

Let us roll all our strength and all

Our sweetness up into one ball,

And tear our pleasures with rough strife

Through the iron gates of life:

Thus, though we cannot make our sun

Stand still, yet we will make him run.

Explore the Theme of Power in Andrew Marvell's *To His Coy Mistress.*

In Andrew Marvell's *To his Coy Mistress*, the speaker attempts to persuade his 'mistress' to sleep with him. The noun 'mistress' could refer to a person with whom he is already having an extra-marital relationship, or it could simply mean that the woman is in a position of authority and control: she is literally the mistress of the situation, wielding power. The fact that the poem is in the form of a formal metaphysical argument suggests, however, that the speaker holds the power: metaphysical poems are highly intellectualised, and this one has a syllogistic structure, which I shall discuss below. The choice of form therefore indicates that the speaker believes he holds the power in their relationship, but the use of the word 'mistress' creates doubt.

On the other hand, the most obvious evidence for the 'mistress' wielding the power can be seen with the adjective 'coy', which to a modern reader means coquettish. By accusing the 'lady' of 'coyness', coupled with the alliterative 'crime', the speaker suggests that she is flirting and playing games with him. This is reinforced through the choice of meter. Although at first glance the first two lines of the poem appear to be in perfect iambic tetrameter, it is possible to read the first two syllables of the second line as a spondee:

/ /   x /   x /   x /

This coy | ness, La | dy, were | no crime,

The spondee creates a cynical and frustrated tone with its emphasis on 'this coy-', implying that the speaker does not believe that her reticence is genuine. Moreover, the spondee emphasises the stressed syllable in '<u>la</u>dy', almost turning the direct address into an accusation or insult.

Another factor that might emphasise the speaker's frustration with the power-wielding lady might be attitudes to pre-marital sex at the time. The poem was written between 1651-2, when Oliver Cromwell and the Puritans ran the country. Under the influence of the Puritans, pre-marital sex was frowned upon; however, according to Brabcová, there was a large gap between theory and reality as 25% of

131

Englishwomen were pregnant when they married.[1] Culturally, this was more accepted than it might seem, as pregnancies confirmed that women were able to bear those all-important heirs. Although Marvell supported Cromwell, the speaker in the poem does not share his Puritan values. Therefore, there is a slender possibility that, bearing the social context in mind, this desire to sleep with the lady might be a precursor to a long-term relationship. The speaker states:

And the last age should show your heart.

For, lady, you deserve this state,

This might hint at a long-term relationship, as the couple might hope for pregnancy and then marriage: 'heart' obviously has connotations of love and perhaps 'state' refers to the marriage state. However, it is significant that her 'heart' is the last body part in his list ('eyes...forehead... breast...the rest...heart'). If she notices this, she is likely to be suspicious of his intentions.

Although the speaker might genuinely believe that the lady holds the power to reject his demands, she might <u>not</u> be a flirt: as mentioned earlier, the abstract adjective 'coy' can mean coquettish, but it can also mean undemonstrative or shy.[2] This interpretation could be supported with his polite term of address ('lady') and the fact that he recognises her 'coyness' might indicate that he respects her feelings. Indeed, he acknowledges them with his references to the ways that he would court her if he had the 'time'. His use of hyperbole ('an hundred years...two hundred...thirty thousand') might be a way of exaggerating his respect for her and the use of enjambment ('Shouldst rubies find; I by the tide/ Of Humber would complain.') adds to the effect of slowing down time. Moreover, in the first stanza, he uses the personal pronoun 'we' twice, followed by 'thou' once and the subject personal pronoun 'you' three times. The personal pronoun 'thou' was used in Shakespearean times to express intimacy while 'you' was used by inferiors to

---

[1] Alice Brabcová, *The Woman's Story,* (Plzeň: University of West Bohemia, n.d.), http://www.phil.muni.cz/angl/thepes/thepes_02_02.pdf [accessed 6 April, 2015]

[2] *The Shorter Oxford English Dictionary on Historical Principles*, ed. by C.T. Onions, 3rd edn, 2 vols (Oxford: Oxford University Press, 1973), p.446

superiors or by the upper classes to each other.[3] The fact that Marvell shifts from 'thou' to 'you' signifies a change of attitude.[4] Perhaps the speaker forgets himself after his attempt at intimacy with 'thou', or perhaps he has received nonverbal feedback of disapproval from the lady (after all, this poem is also a dramatic monologue), suggesting that he has overstepped the mark, hence the shift to 'you', with some slippage into 'thine' and 'thy' with the romantic 'praise/Thine eyes, and on thy forehead gaze'. Interestingly, he only uses the subject personal pronoun 'I' three times in this stanza, perhaps illustrating that the 'lady' is very much the focus of the speaker's attention. The romantic tone is rather spoilt, however, with the pun 'my vegetable love should grow', which could be a metaphor for the male or female anatomy. Puns such as this, coupled with the theme of *carpe diem* is characteristic of metaphysical poetry.[5] The speaker is being too clever, and the reader begins to realise that his professions of love might not be as they first seem.

Moreover, an examination of other poems written by Marvell supports the idea that women hold the power. His three Mower poems (*Damon the Mower, The Mower to the Glo-Worms* and *The Mower's Song*) express Damon's frustration at the rejection of his advances by a certain 'fair Shepherdess', Juliana. This feeling of being hurt and aggrieved is voiced in all of the Mower poems.[6] Moreover, in Marvell's *The Unfortunate Lover*, the knight is in a condition of endlessly frustrated hope as cormorants 'fed him up with Hopes and Air, / Which soon digested to Despair' while in *The Definition of Love*, the lovers are compared to opposite poles of the earth, so 'can never meet'. If we bear the sentiment of Marvell's other poems in mind, perhaps we can conclude that the speaker in *To his Coy Mistress* knows that he has no hope of consummating their relationship, but he is resolved to keep trying.

---

[3] David Crystal and Ben Crystal, *Explore Shakespeare's Works*, (Penguin Books Limited, 2008), http://www.shakespeareswords.com/thou-and-you [accessed 13 April, 2015].

[4] Ibid.

[5] *Metaphysical Poetry: Definition, Characteristics & Examples*, (Study.com, 2003), http://study.com/academy/lesson/metaphysical-poetry-definition-characteristics-examples.html [accessed 13 April, 2015].

[6] The Poetry Foundation, http://www.poetryfoundation.org/bio/andrew-marvell [accessed 6 April, 2015]

Another layer of power, however, is that of manipulation. When we examine the language and meter of the poem in more detail, we realise that the power to manipulate is more likely to be in the hands of the speaker. Earlier, we analysed the use of spondee in the second line of the first stanza. An alternative way of reading the first two lines is as perfect iambic tetrameter:


```
x  /   x  /   x  /    x  /
```

Had we | but world | enough, | and time,

```
 x  /   x   / x   /   x  /
```

This coy | ness, La | dy, were | no crime,

The regular iambic feet could imply that he is deliberately attempting to harmonise or agree with the woman's point of view, creating a regretful tone. This is emphasised with the rhyming couplet 'time' and 'crime', which evokes the feeling that the speaker and the lady are united against the common enemy of time. In addition, the commas slow the pace, especially when the speaker directly addresses the 'lady', singling her out as the sole object of his attention, presumably with the intention to flatter. Moreover, the long vowel sounds in 'world', 'time' and 'no crime' slow the pace, again suggesting that he is agreeing that her 'coy' behaviour is correct and proper. Of course, this is a manipulative strategy: from the syllogistic structure of the poem, the Cambridge-educated Marvell would know full well that if he appears to agree with her and uses this as a starting point, she is likely to listen to the rest of his argument.

The syllogistic structure of the poem also emphasises the speaker's attempts to wield power over the 'lady'. The first stanza is the major premise ('Had we...'), in which he makes his proposition. The second stanza is the minor premise ('But') and the third is the conclusion ('Now therefore'). Ironically, in the minor premise, the speaker talks about time being the enemy ('Time's wingèd chariot hurrying near') and he attempts to frighten the 'lady' into sleeping with him with images of the 'grave'.   But the structure of the poem indicates that he has had the leisure to craft his argument carefully, suggesting that not only does he have a clever and manipulative mind, but that he exploits time to suit his needs. In addition, the poem is in iambic tetrameter, which was unusual for the time as there was a literary tradition of using iambic pentameter.[7] Dropping a metrical foot creates the effect of quickening the pace and increasing pressure on the 'lady' to sleep with him. This calculating behaviour can also be seen in Marvell's poem *Daphnis and Chloe* in which 'coy' Chloe finally offers to sleep with Daphis after he declares that he will no longer court her. He then refuses her advances and cruelly informs her that he has slept with 'Phlogis' and that night will be sleeping with 'Dorinda'. Therefore, not only is the power of education exploited in both poems, but in the latter, the power of psychological abuse is also employed, leading the reader, who is aware of the context, to mistrust further the speaker in *To his Coy Mistress*.

More evidence of the speaker's attempts to exploit the theme of time to exercise power can be seen through the use of rhyming couplets throughout the entire poem. These follow the first couplet (analysed above) to create a momentum, which emphasises the urgency of the speaker's feelings, as he pressurises the 'lady' to 'sport us while we may'. This hedonistic desire to seize the day (*carpe diem*) is seen with the desire to 'tear our pleasures with rough strife', with 'tear' and 'rough' having worrying connotations of violence. The violent imagery might be explained by the backdrop of the English Civil War: Marvell was surrounded by the threat of death and was consequently aware that life was short. However, he missed four years of the war when he was travelling in Europe, and no-one knows what he was doing there: some people thought that he was avoiding the war'.[8] If this is true, it might provide more evidence of his terror of dying and his desire to make the most of life by to seizing the day.

The structure of the poem might even emphasise the speaker's power over his 'mistress'. Most women in Shakespeare's times were not as educated as men: there was the belief that too much learning could endanger a woman's social life and morality[9]. It is therefore possible that she is unable to see the extent to which she is being manipulated.

---

[7] Poemshape, *Why do Poets write Iambic Pentameter?*
https://poemshape.wordpress.com/2009/04/17/why-do-poets-write-iambic-pentameter/
[accessed 6 April, 2015]

[8] The Poetry Foundation.

[9] Miriam Balmuth, 'Female Education in 16th & 17th Century England: Influences, Attitudes, and Trends' *Canadian Woman Studies/Les Cahiers de la Femme* 9, numbers, 17-20, p. 19,
http://pi.library.yorku.ca/ojs/index.php/cws/article/viewFile/11719/10802 [accessed 6 April, 2015]

Perhaps the poem is not meant to be about power at all. T'.S Eliot praises Marvell's wit and proposes that *To his Coy Mistress* is ironic.[10] Despite the poor education that women had in the 17th century, it could be that the 'lady' had enough sense to see the poem was not intended to be taken seriously. She might have recognised the conditional '[h]ad we but world enough and time' in the major premise. Any woman would be offended with the '[b]ut' at the start of the minor premise. This, coupled with the horrific imagery of 'worms shall try/That long-preserved virginity' might put her off altogether, or trigger a response of hysterical laughter. We have to remember that a characteristic of metaphysical poetry is that it contained a lot of wit[11], so the speaker's desire to impress the 'lady' would be all the greater if we consider that 'coyness' in the 17th century had an additional meaning of being deliberately aloof.[12] It would create a feeling of great intellectual satisfaction for Marvell if his wit could provoke a response from a disdainful lady.

In conclusion, the question of who holds the power essentially breaks down to the power of persuasion, the power to flirt, the power to be resolute and the power to provoke. If we also consider the power of wit, this would serve a reminder to the modern reader that our forefathers also had a sense of humour. Perhaps we should bear this in mind when interpreting poems from the past.

Useful Tip!

If you want to check that your essay has the clear thread of discussion needed to gain a good AO1 mark, copy it to a new file and then delete everything except the topic sentences. They should reveal a well signposted response with a good developing argument.

Below are the topic sentences from the essay that you have just read; the key word has been highlighted in **red**, or notes have been made in brackets.

---

[10] T.S. Eliot, *Selected Essays: New Edition*, (New York: Harcourt, Brace and World, 1950), pp. 251-263.

[11] *Metaphysical Poetry: Definition, Characteristics & Examples.*

[12] *The Shorter Oxford English Dictionary*

1. In Andrew Marvell's 'To his Coy Mistress', the speaker attempts to persuade his 'mistress' to sleep with him. *(Power is implied.)*

2. On the other hand, the most obvious evidence for the 'mistress' wielding the **power** can be seen with the adjective 'coy', which to a modern reader means coquettish.

3. Another factor that might emphasise the speaker's frustration with the **power-wielding** lady might be attitudes to pre-marital sex at the time.

4. Although the speaker might genuinely believe that the lady holds the **power** to reject his demands, she might <u>not</u> be a flirt: as mentioned earlier, the abstract adjective 'coy' can mean coquettish, but it can also mean undemonstrative or shy.

5. Moreover, an examination of other poems written by Marvell supports the idea that women hold the **power**.

6. Another layer of **power**, however, is that of manipulation.

7. The syllogistic structure of the poem also emphasises the speaker's attempts to wield **power** over the 'lady'.

8. More evidence of the speaker's attempts to exploit the theme of time to exercise **power** can be seen through the use of rhyming couplets throughout the entire poem.

The structure of the poem might even emphasise the speaker's **power** over his 'mistress'.

9. Perhaps the poem is not meant to be about **power** at all.

10. In conclusion, the question of who holds the **power** essentially breaks down to the **power** of persuasion, the **power** to flirt, the **power** to be resolute and the **power** to provoke.

Finally...

We hope that this guide has helped you to understand the skills and knowledge needed to attain your potential in your A' level in English literature.

If you have found this guide useful, please feel free to post a review on Amazon. Mr Bruff (@MrBruffEnglish) and I (@Mrs_SPaG) would love to hear you get on.

In the meantime, good luck with your A' level in English Literature!

Printed in Great Britain
by Amazon